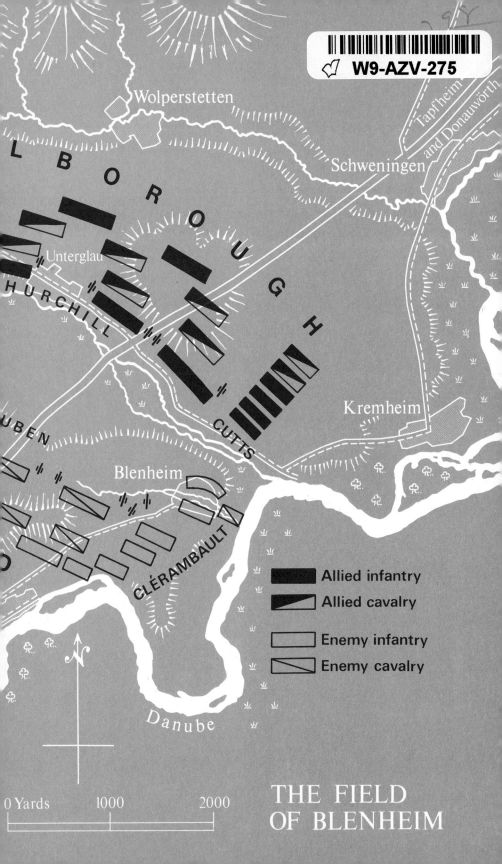

W9-AZV-275

Wolperstetten

Tapheim and Donauwörth

Schweningen

LBOROUGH

Unterglau

HURCHILL

UBEN

CUTTS

Kremheim

Blenheim

CLÉRAMBAULT

Allied infantry

Allied cavalry

Enemy infantry

Enemy cavalry

Danube

0 Yards 1000 2000

THE FIELD
OF BLENHEIM

BLENHEIM

BLENHEIM

David Green

CHARLES SCRIBNER'S SONS

NEW YORK

ISBN 0-684-14128-0

Printed in Great Britain

Library of Congress Catalog Card Number 74-16822

Contents

Illustrations

ILLUSTRATIONS

Maps

Author's Notes

Method of Dating. Until 1752 the English at home always used the Old Style of dating, after 1700 eleven days behind the New Style of Gregory XIII's Calendar, current in all Continental countries except Russia. Our soldiers in the Netherlands and Germany generally used the New Style, which accordingly has, unless otherwise stated, been adopted throughout this book. Until recent times the quitrent banner for Blenheim Palace, due every year at Windsor on the anniversary of the battle of Blenheim, was still being delivered on August 2nd. It is now sent on August 13th.

Place Names. Although the village in Bavaria where the battle was fought was and is called Blindheim, it has long since in England been known as Blenheim and is therefore so named in this book. I have ventured too to shorten the names of the neighbouring villages of Oberglauheim and Unterglauheim to Oberglau and Unterglau. Maps also of course have changed since 1704 when Holland was a state of the United Provinces, Spain owned the Spanish Netherlands (now Belgium), and Austria was, with the small German states, part of the Holy Roman Empire.

English and British. The Union between England and Scotland was brought about three years after the battle of Blenheim. Our troops who fought in it were usually referred to collectively as the English; although, as will be seen from the list of regiments given at page 149, many of them were Scots, Irish or Welsh.

Introduction

Fame has its fashions. Two and a half centuries after his death Marlborough, blackened by Macaulay, whitewashed by Churchill, today, in the world's estimation, stands serene as his stylito statue in Blenheim Park: that Column of Victory, raised by his widow, to endure, like his fame, 'for as long as the British name and language shall last'.

From that column ranks of elms stretch to the horizon, as did the long, opposing lines at the battle of Blenheim. And at Blindheim too, beside the Danube, as the mind's eye strains to encompass the scene, it comes sooner or later to focus on Marlborough, ever calm amid chaos as he 'rides in the whirlwind and directs the storm'.

Of his other qualities none had more instant appeal than his daring, that gargantuan impudence with which he bluffed allies and enemy, strode across Europe, stormed the Schellenberg, won Blenheim and then packed a marshal of France into his coach. This, thought every would-be hero of Queen Anne's day, was how a great man and a great general should behave. But was he not more than that? In his audacity and foresight, in his serenity and invincibility – to say nothing of his appearance, 'handsome as an angel' – might he not be regarded as a god? Admittedly, from the Court of St James's to Olympus was a biggish step, yet not too big surely to be taken in this conqueror's stride.

And so it is that among the gods painted on the ceilings of Blenheim Palace we see Marlborough looking as much at home as he does among his officers in the tapestries beneath them. As Lediard put it, he won all the battles he fought and was 'ever beloved by his own soldiers and dreaded by those of the enemy'.

As for his patience - with his wife, with the Dutch, with every kind of frustration from blinding headaches to recalcitrant allies - one can only see it as in scale with the rest. Naturally, he was supported by the officers he deserved - Cadogan and Cutts, Orkney and Ingoldsby: English, Irish, Scots with fire in their bellies; and none more valiant than his collaborator in battle, Prince Eugene of Savoy.

His common soldiers were then called the dregs of humanity. Many of them were gaol-birds. It was not the least part of his genius that he recognised them as human beings and from the ore that he found in them forged a sword of invincible steel.

I

PRELUDE

But as too prolix Accounts of Actions, tho' never so Glorious and Memorable, are generally tedious to most Readers, I have endeavour'd every where to bring them within as narrow a Compass as the Circumstances of Affairs would admit.

THOMAS LEDIARD
The Life of John Duke of Marlborough (1736)

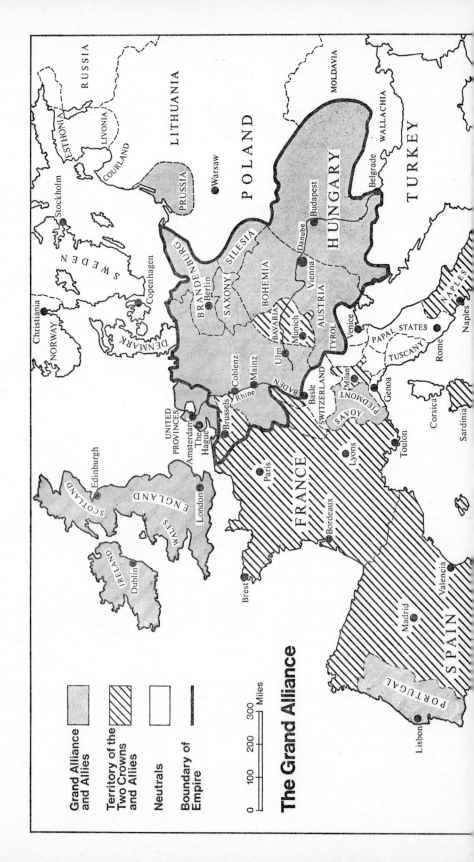

The Grand Alliance

1

Over the Hills and Far Away

Now tell us all about the war
And what they fought each other for.
SOUTHEY, *After Blenheim*

On the coldest day for years, in the middle of January 1704, Marlborough sailed to the Hague to tell the government of Holland, in confidence, of his plan to invade France through the Moselle valley. This alarmed them. They could not, they felt, afford to take risks with their army; their own frontiers, threatened by France, must come first.

Marlborough, still at the Hague in February, wrote to Sarah his duchess: 'For this campaign I see so very ill a prospect that I am extremely out of heart. But God's will be done. In all the other campaigns I had an opinion of being able to do something for the common cause, but in this I have no other hopes than that some lucky accident may enable me to do good.'

From one whose motto was Faithful But Unfortunate this perhaps was to be taken as little more than a gesture to disarm Providence, for never was there a general who left so little to chance. Within seven months his hopes were fulfilled on the field of Blenheim.

*

On her accession in 1702 Queen Anne had found a war ready prepared for her. William, her predecessor, had with Louis XIV done much to try to avoid it by agreeing who should succeed to the Spanish throne. But Death itself seemed to be

15

working against them, snatching first, in 1699, the young
Bavarian Joseph Ferdinand, chosen to succeed Charles II
of Spain as ruler of the Spanish Empire, and then in the
following year Charles himself who, in his will, named as
his heir and successor Louis XIV's grandson Philip.

Louis hesitated before agreeing to that nomination. It
meant dishonouring the Treaty of Ryswick and would almost certainly lead to war; but the alternative was to support the other young candidate we were backing for the
Spanish throne – Archduke Charles, the younger son of the
Emperor Leopold – and Louis had no wish to make Spain
and her vast possessions farflung parts of the Holy Roman
Empire. So Louis accepted the will and in 1701, on the death
of our exiled King James II, made peace still more precarious
by acknowledging James's son, James Francis Edward (the
Old Pretender), as the rightful King of England.

This was bad enough for England, but the very thought
of France and Spain united under one crown was repugnant
and daunting to the rest of Europe. Spain's territories then
included the Spanish Netherlands, a large part of Italy and
huge territories in America, not forgetting the highly
profitable slave-trade called the Asiento, soon to be made
over to France. World markets were at risk for England,
Holland (the United Provinces) and for Leopold's Empire
with its capital in Vienna: the Grand Alliance which William, with Marlborough's help, had had the wisdom to
found in 1701. On March 8th 1702 William died.

On April 23rd 1702 Anne was crowned; on May 4th, in
consequence of the new threats, war was declared against
France. Our chief allies were the Dutch and Leopold's
Austrians, while Danes, Hanoverians, Prussians, Hessians
and other confederates, as they were called, were to join us
later.

Marlborough's first action was to clear the Rhine and
Maas valleys of the French, in the first summer of the war,

an achievement without which the campaign culminating in Blenheim would not have been possible.

In September 1702 Max Emmanuel, Electoral Prince of Bavaria, sided with France. Gallant, ambitious, impulsive, he was believed to be aiming to snatch Leopold's crown; and certainly, by the position of Bavaria in the bowels of his empire, this defection put Vienna, capital of the Holy Roman Empire, in peril. It did in fact nearly fall in the summer of 1703. Luckily for Leopold, the two enemy commanders, Marshal Villars and the Elector of Bavaria, had then fallen out. Villars was recalled and replaced by the far less brilliant Marshal Marsin, who was to oppose us at Blenheim.

Vienna's peril, however, was only temporarily reduced. On the east it was seriously threatened by Rakoczy's Hungarian revolt, backed by France; while on the Rhine Marshal Tallard, at Strasbourg, was preparing to reinforce the Elector and Marsin, near Ulm, with 36,000 men by marching them through the Black Forest. To defend his capital all Leopold could count on were 36,000 Imperialists under Prince Louis of Baden in the Lines of Stollhofen, near Strasbourg, and a further 10,000 under Count Styrum, observing the Danube town of Ulm.

All this to Englishmen living at that time (there were fewer than six million of them) could be confusing; and after all, who in England cared for remote dynasties or for risking their lives to rescue Vienna? Still, there was usually some handy phrase for summing things up, and in this case war was said to be necessary to curb the exorbitant power of France. That was understandable. From the Queen down, in fact, it appealed to everybody and gave rise to the proper amount of indignation. Louis was too big for his boots, and so were those 'haughty, towering Monsieurs' about him.

In any case to the English soldier, as often as not, the cause mattered less than the commanding officer; and as for the auxiliaries, paid by us or by the Dutch to swell the polyglot army, they could if need be in their various tongues persuade themselves, as the French and the Bavarians would be doing, that theirs was a righteous war. Luckily, England had the money to pay them. True, many of her own servants – ministers, ambassadors and so on – were two years or more in arrears with their salaries, but the relative prosperity of England was still the envy of her allies – more especially of Vienna and the Empire, which looked like heading for bankruptcy – and of her enemies.

Even now no one knows exactly when Marlborough's mind vaulted from the Moselle to the Danube, nor who influenced him most in that tremendous decision. Archdeacon Coxe, the nineteenth-century biographer of Marlborough, wrote of pleading letters from Prince Eugene of Savoy, in the archives at Blenheim Palace. No one since has been able to find them. What is certain however is that Count Johann Wratislaw, the Emperor Leopold's Ambassador in London, had during 1703 repeatedly begged Marlborough to rescue Vienna, and that by the beginning of April 1704 Marlborough had secretly agreed to march in that cause to the Danube. He had suffered so much from the caution and restraint of the Dutch Field-Deputies that he told Wratislaw he would rather lead thirty English battalions into Germany than stay in the Low Countries in command of the English in that Anglo-Dutch army.

Those in the know or even partly in the know were a very small group indeed. They included Queen Anne and her Consort Prince George of Denmark, and the Lord Treasurer, Sidney Lord Godolphin, to whom Marlbrough imparted the secret on April 29th. Even Sarah, Marlborough's duchess, was not told until later. The political climate in England, with Tories like Nottingham favouring a limited sea-war, was far from favourable; and had the project been debated in Parliament, not only would it probably have been rejected, but all the world would have known of it. As things were, the French secret service, though not as good as Marlborough's, was not to be underestimated. (On a wall of the Saloon in Blenheim Palace Sarah was later to have spies depicted with outsize ears.) If the master-plan was not to be abortive, they must be kept guessing as nearly as possible to the last ditch.

Queen Anne may not fully have grasped the need for that 'long, laborious march' to the Danube, but she had a profound confidence in the general she knew as Mr Freeman. In his youth, as John Churchill, a guardsman trained under Turenne, it would have been easy to underestimate him and to write him off as a typical product of the court of Charles II, drifting as he did from one of Charles's mistresses, Barbara Castlemaine, to a younger beauty, Sarah Jennings, who in the course of courtship sent scathing letters and made her own terms, including marriage, for total surrender.

There was never a more cynical age. The Dorset home where Churchill had been born in 1650 was a house divided against itself; his father Sir Winston a fighting royalist, his maternal grandmother, in whose house they lived, stubbornly Cromwellian. With such a background it must almost have amounted to second nature to keep a foot in each camp: to leave James II for William III and yet intrigue with the old master while serving the new. Nothing was clearcut. Today's king might be tomorrow's exile, today's enemy tomorrow's ally. The Duke of Berwick, fighting for France (though not at Blenheim) against Marlborough, his uncle and friend, was the son of Arabella, Marlborough's sister, and of James II. Prince Eugene, Marlborough's partner at Blenheim, was an Italian nobleman, born and trained in France.

To be ambitious, as Churchill undoubtedly was, meant walking delicately and, not once but often, gambling with one's very life. It can hardly have surprised him to find himself, in the reign of William and Mary, a prisoner in the

Tower; nor, years after Mary's death, was he astonished when the same King William made him Governor to young Gloucester, the ill-starred son of the future Queen Anne. With Anne, Churchill and his wife had for years been in high favour, and when in 1702 she came to the throne she gave him the Garter, while making Sarah Groom of the Stole and Mistress of the Robes.

In his military career Churchill advanced steadily from 'a pair of colours in the Foot Guards' in the reign of Charles II to the top rank of Captain General and Master General of the Ordnance, under Anne. Even so, as Mr Chandler points out, he was never, like Wellington or Napoleon, supreme commander, nor enjoyed true freedom of action, but was 'precariously dependent on the support of the politicians at the Hague and Westminster.' His 1702-3 campaigns on the Rhine and the Maas, while they had earned him his dukedom, gave little indication of what was to come.

*

On the 19th of April 1704, after a short and busy visit to England, Marlborough embarked at Harwich, for the Hague, with his brother General Charles Churchill, Count Wratislaw, the Earl of Orkney and other officers. Sarah his duchess took coach to Harwich for the leave-taking, and a more disheartening send-off never was known. Fourteen months before, their only surviving son, Lord Blandford, had at the age of seventeen died from smallpox. Sarah was now forty-four and, though still hoping for a male heir (there were four daughters), recently had had doubts not only of herself, but of Marlborough as a faithful husband. She accused him of infidelity with an unnamed woman, now thought to have been Lady Southwell, and the more he denied it the more she chose to disbelieve him. On the quayside, as he left for the most hazardous campaign of his life, she handed him a paper full of her accusations, a diatribe so violent and bitter that, after reading it, he said he no longer cared if he lived or died.

Luckily, once he had gone, something happened to change her attitude and she sent after him an express of a quite different tone. She even suggested joining him in the campaign. Replying from the Hague he told her:

I do this minute love you better than ever I did before . . . What you propose as to coming over I should be extremely pleased with, for your letter has so transported me . . . although I should not be able to see you often, but . . . I am going up into Germany, where it would be impossible for you to follow me; but love me as you now do and no hurt can come to me. You have by this kindness preserved my quiet and I believe my life, for till I had this letter I had been very indifferent of what should become of myself. I have pressed this business of carrying an army into Germany in order to leave a good name behind me, wishing for nothing else but good success. I shall now add that of having a long life, that I may be happy with you.

'This business of carrying an army into Germany' was of course what had chiefly occupied his mind during the winter: how to persuade the Dutch to let him take troops even to the Moselle, let alone the Danube, when they saw themselves invaded by France directly his back was turned. Queen Anne, with their support, had made him Commander of all the English (though not the Dutch) Land Forces in the Netherlands, as well as Master-General of the Ordnance. Why desert them now? It was not for him to remind them of all the obstacles flung in his path by their Field-Deputies when he had planned to get to grips with the enemy in the last campaign.

On May 1st Marlborough firmly told the Dutch he had decided to march to the Moselle with all the troops in English pay, leaving Field Marshal Overkirk with enough men to protect them and to come racing back himself with troops brought by a fleet of barges down the Rhine, should the French, under Villeroi (Louis XIV's marshal, defending the northern front and watching the lower Rhine), fail to follow his trail. The Dutch, though still thinking it too early in the season for such a march, yielded with a good grace, and indeed from then on seemed eager to co-operate.

Once the go-ahead had been given, Operation Danube, disguised as Operation Moselle, could get under way. With the help of his secretary, Adam Cardonnel, and a small handful of officers, Marlborough made provision for everything from coaches to cannonballs, including pontoons for river-crossings and waggons for bread, for artillery and for transporting the wounded. Heavy waggons for artillery were of course essential; but for the lighter jobs Marlborough himself had designed a small, two-wheeled cart, lightly sprung and drawn by two horses. The French called it a *Marlbrouk*. Physicians, surgeons, apothecaries, all would be needed. So would chaplains, led by the Chaplain-General, Francis Hare. The infantry would be under the command of his brother, General Charles Churchill; and the artillery under Colonel Blood, whose father had so nearly succeeded in stealing the crown jewels. Most important of all - money. This would be controlled from London by the Marlboroughs' closest friend, Lord Treasurer Godolphin, from Frankfurt by Henry Davenant and from Amsterdam by Benjamin Sweet, Paymaster to Her Majesty's Forces in the Low Countries.

A few days previously, on April 28th, Marlborough had written from Holland to his duchess, 'I am hagged out of my life, so that I long extremely for Monday when I intend to leave this place'; and next day to Godolphin, 'My intentions are to march with all the English to Coblenz and to declare that I intend to campaign on the Moselle; but when I come there, to write to the (Dutch) States that I think it absolutely necessary for the saving of the Empire to march with the troops under my command and to join with those that are in Germany that are in Her Majesty's and the Dutch pay, in order to take measures with Prince Louis of Baden for the speedy reduction of the Elector of Bavaria. What I now write I beg may be known to nobody but Her Majesty and the Prince.'

2

The Red Caterpillar

Courage, boys, 'tis one to ten
That we return all gentlemen,
While conquering colours we display,
Over the hills and far away.
        Contemporary marching song

As Marlborough's army set out from Breda for a rendezvous at Bedburg, whence the main march started on May 12th, the predominant colour was red: the red caterpillar, as Sir Winston Churchill called it; though how long it would remain so was another question. Mud and dust permitting, officers' coats continued colourful; but for the rank and file, once out in the country, they turned theirs inside out, to save them for reviews and to be sure of making a brave show on parade. At this date, when the uniform for each regiment was often chosen by its colonel, cheapness and comfort came before smartness. Generally speaking, the English favoured red, the Dutch blue and the Imperialists under Prince Eugene, green; and those are the colours in which contemporary tapestries and frescoes show them fighting.

Adam Cardonnel estimated the strength as 'upwards of 40,000 men (40 battalions of infantry and 80 squadrons of cavalry),* very good troops', which France would 'not be able to match for goodness'. And certainly very good they became, whatever they were like when first recruited.

---

* Theoretically a battalion, at this date, mustered 700, a squadron 150; in practice the numbers were usually nearer 500 for a battalion and, for a squadron, 120. Field armies usually marched in a series of columns, with artillery in the centre and supply-waggons in the rear. Marlborough took 1,700 supply-waggons drawn by 5,000 draught-horses.

Writing of officers Bishop Burnet says: 'The Duke of Marlborough's army was beyond all contradiction the best academy in the world to teach a young gentleman wit and breeding; a sot and a drunkard being what they scorned.' Of the other ranks he says they too often began at a disadvantage; and yet even for them there could be hope of redemption: 'The poor soldiers who were (too many of them) the refuse and dregs of the nation became after one or two campaigns, by the care of their officers and by good order and discipline, tractable, civil, orderly, sensible and clean and had an air and a spirit above the vulgar.' At all fixed camps, he goes on to say, (themselves 'like a quiet and well-governed city and perhaps much more mannerly'), prayers were said morning and evening 'and on Sundays with sermons'. On top of which, Marlborough himself was 'so great a discourager of vice as to give particular directions to the Provost-Marshal to chase away all lewd women from about his quarters'.

This would strongly have appealed to Lieutenant-Colonel Blackader of the Cameronians (then Ferguson's Regiment), singing hymns and psalms as he marched, though already, at the outset, 'weary of the tents of sin'. The army, he reflected, was a sad place to be in on the Sabbath when, for all Burnet said to the contrary (and after all, he was not there), 'nothing was to be heard but cursing and swearing'. Blackader notes in his journal moments of despair when he feels he can no longer endure 'the scum and dregs of mankind, who seem like devils broke loose from Hell'. But then with divine help he recovers and praises God and tells Him, 'For my own part I am not anxious . . . and whatever Thou dost with the English army, I am persuaded that by Thy mercy I shall set up my Ebenezers* through Germany.' In the meantime, singing his way – in competition with *Lilliburlero* and *Over the Hills and Far Away* – from Bedburg to

* Ebenezer: the memorial stone set up by Samuel after the victory of Mizpeh. (I Samuel, vii, 12)

25

Coblenz, where he nearly drowned in the Moselle, Blackader told himself, 'This is like to be a campaign of great fatigue and trouble. I know not where they are leading us . . .'

Nor did the French. Where on earth was Marlborough bound for? Deserters kept telling them the Moselle. Could they be heading for Strasbourg or for Landau? Villeroi at first believed that Marlborough had no intention of crossing the Rhine; for taking that way he must pass across the fronts of two French armies and stretch his lines of communication along the Rhine, where the left bank in its central reaches was in French hands. Villeroi appealed to Versailles. 'If Marlborough himself marches to the Moselle', Louis answered, 'you too must march.'

Soon after Marlborough's march had begun English politicians suggested he had stolen the army; while the Dutch panicked at the prospect of Villeroi's attacking them; but Marlborough remained calm. The bait had been taken. Villeroi marched to Trèves, to 'observe' our army. Was Strasbourg its objective? By ordering the Governor of Phillippsburg to build bridges of boats there across the river, Marlborough might be said to have been doing Villeroi's thinking for him. He almost certainly had no notion of marching that way. Tallard too was puzzled and postponed marching his main army to Ulm until he had had fresh instructions from Versailles.

Marlborough had bargained for all this: for the time-lag caused by the slow pace at which news then travelled and by Louis XIV's insistence upon his generals' referring every-thing back to Versailles before action was taken. It took one to three days for the French marshals to hear of Marl-borough's movements and when they did hear, instead of advancing to counter them, they wasted more time by seeking their King's directions. That Marlborough's objec-tive might possibly be the Danube was among their guesses, but a guess was not good enough when, as seemed equally likely, France's own frontiers might be threatened; and by

Marlborough on his magnificent grey at the battle of Blenheim

Queen Anne

Louis XIV

Sarah, Duchess of Marlborough

The Emperor Leopold

A 'Marlbrouk', one of the supply carts designed by Marlborough.
A sergeant of the Royal Scots with his halberd keeps the civilian
driver to his post

the time the Danube had begun to look like a certainty, it was too late to stop him. As on other occasions Marlborough took the initiative and at the same time took pains to see that he was at least one move ahead.

On May 26th Marlborough reached Coblenz, where supplies had been marshalled and where 5,000 Hanoverians and Prussians joined the strength. The Moselle had been crossed and, on the 27th, the Rhine by two bridges of boats. 'There will be no campaign on the Moselle,' Villeroi wrote to Louis, 'the English have all gone higher up into Germany.' They were followed by Dutch reinforcements of seven battalions and twenty-two squadrons.

Heading south-eastwards, through the state of Hesse-Cassel where the Hereditary Prince joined them, Marlborough's men marched on not, as one might imagine, always in strict step to a drum-beat but, as one sees in the Blenheim tapestries, easily, almost casually. Along the mud roads of Germany, in a wet May, they kept up their easy pace, in drab coats and three-cornered hats, with swords, flintlocks* and packs; swearing, singing, learning to like the beer, the wine and the women, 'some of them', as Lieutenant Pope declared, 'much handsomer than we expected to find in this country.'

The march, in many ways remarkable, was not especially so for speed; even though, for that purpose, siege-guns were not included in the artillery train. From Bedburg to Ulm (less than 300 miles) took them forty-one days. For the first eleven days General Churchill and the infantry kept up an average of between eleven and twelve miles a day, but before the crossing of the Neckar they were several days' march behind Marlborough and the cavalry and had to be waited for. However, for the first half of the march speed

---

* 'By 1700 the standard infantry firearm in the English forces was the flintlock musket – the predecessor of the famed "Brown Bess" – a far more reliable weapon than the ancient matchlock it replaced. The latter however lingered on in the French service for some years. A second important development was the growing employment of the ring bayonet.' Chandler: *The Marlborough Wars*, Appendix I.

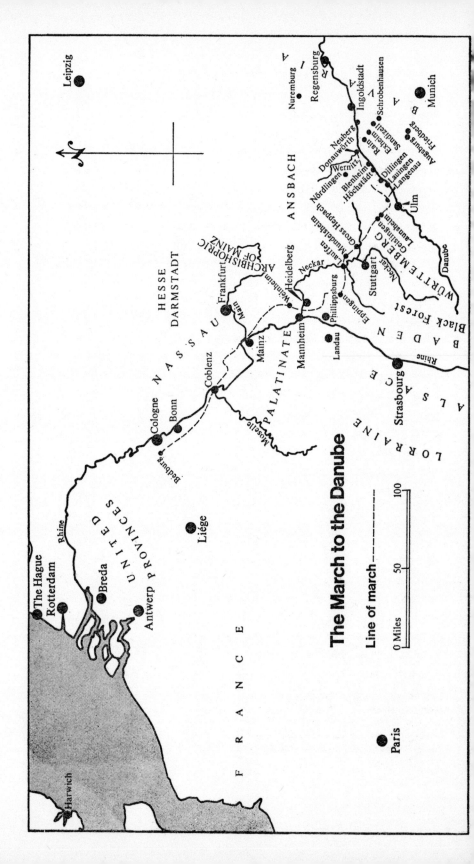

The March to the Danube

Line of march - - - - - -

0 Miles   50   100

Harwich

The Hague
Rotterdam
Breda
Antwerp
Liége
Paris

UNITED PROVINCES

FRANCE

Rhine

Bedburg
Cologne
Bonn
Coblenz

NASSAU

HESSE
DARMSTADT

Leipzig

Frankfurt
Weinheim
Heidelberg
Mainz

ARCHBISHOPRIC
OF MAINZ

Main
Neckar

PALATINATE

Mannheim
Phillippsburg
Landau
Eppingen

Moselle

LORRAINE

ALSACE

Strasbourg

Rhine

BADEN

Black Forest

WÜRTEMBERG

Stuttgart
Neckar
Gross Heppach
Mundelsheim
Lauffen
Gesslingen
Launsheim
Ulm
Langenau
Lauingen
Dillingen
Höchstädt
Blenheim
Nördlingen
Wernitz
Donauwörth
Neuberg
Rain
Exheim
Sandizell
Schrobenhausen
Friedesg
Ausburg

ANSBACH

Danube

Nuremburg
Regensburg
Ingoldstadt
Munich

was not vital, and the pace had not been set as it would have been today.

At Mainz the Elector, who had sent Marlborough his 'flying (floating) bridge' to help with river-crossings and had been asked to review the infantry, expressed surprise at their handsome appearance; they obviously having had notice to smarten themselves up. 'But when His Highness came to Her Majesty's battalion of Guards, which there consisted of above 700 able men, he seemed to view each man from head to foot and, observing not only their order but the cleanliness of their arms, accoutrements, clothes, shoes and linen, said: "A coup sûr, tous ces messieurs sont habillés pour le bal".' Marlborough of course was gratified. 'Notwithstanding the continual marching', he wrote from Mainz to Godolphin, 'the men are extremely pleased with this expedition, so that I am sure you will take all the care possible that they may not want.' Captain Robert Parker, who was one of them, wrote in his journal:

When we had passed the Rhine the Duke, for the convenience of forage, advanced a day's march and took his rout with the Horse [cavalry] different from that of the Foot [infantry], which was left under the command of General Churchill. We frequently marched three, sometimes four days successively and [then] halted a day. We generally began our march about three in the morning, proceeded about four leagues or four and a half each day and reached our ground about nine. As we marched through the countries of our allies, commissaries were appointed to furnish us with all manner of necessaries for man and horse. These were brought to the ground before we arrived and the soldiers had nothing to do but to pitch their tents, boil their kettles and lie down to rest. Surely never was such a march carried on with more order and regularity and with less fatigue both to man and horse.

In short, if a soldier behaved himself, as most of them did, he could expect a fair deal. It was tough going of course, but less tough than under other commands, where kettledrums might be commoner than kettles. In any case they would not be brewing tea. Indian tea had yet to be heard of and China tea cost Queen Anne £2 a pound. Even so, British soldiers have never had to be taught how to make themselves at home in a foreign country.

On the other hand, in an army where not a few of the recruits had been gaolbirds, or had been recruited (many of them in Ireland) as an alternative to gaol, discipline needed to be severe. In the Camp Reports at Blenheim one reads: 'If any soldiers are found plundering or marauding, they shall be hanged without mercy'. 'No women to be seen with the Lines, but to go all to the rear of the English Train (of artillery)'. And again, 'The woman taken up putting off false coin or money, to be whipped at the head of the Line tomorrow, in case she won't discover her associates'.

Who were these women? Some would be sutlers, supplying those who could afford them with extras to supplement dull rations. Some would be camp-followers or *vivandières* like Mother Ross, prepared to loot the dead of their clothes. Others, married to soldiers, were soon to be widowed and to become nurses. We shall hear more of them later.

Until now all armies in this Cockpit of Europe had reckoned to live off the country, whether it belonged to friend or foe. Marlborough changed that practice. Each major was to tell his company man by man that if one of them stole anything from the peasants bringing in provisions, 'were it but an egg', he would be hanged. If however at a court-martial held en route the sentence of death was passed, there might still be a fifty-fifty chance of a pardon. Camp Reports give more than one case where with two offenders so sentenced they were ordered to draw lots, the loser to hang, the winner to be pardoned and returned to his regiment. A dragoon named John Yeoman, found guilty of insulting his superior officer, Quartermaster Scott, was sentenced to 'run the gantelope (gauntlet) three times through the regiment'.

'Oh that God might reform this army', exclaimed Blackader, 'that good men might have some pleasure in it'. Perhaps 'when the carcases of the one half of us are dung on the earth in Germany', the other half might come to its senses. In the meanwhile it was 'a sad thing to be in an army where one has not confidence to pray for success'. In his view indeed they didn't deserve it.

Marlborough's musings were of a different order. His guessing-game was ending. Sarah, told of his plans, had again offered to join him and had again been gently discouraged. Writing to her from Weinheim on June 2nd he speaks of his longing to be with his family in the riverside house in Hertfordshire: 'I am now in a house of the Elector Palatine that has a prospect over the finest country that is possible to be seen. I see out of my chamber window the Rhine and the Neckar, and his two principal towns of Mannheim and Heidelberg, but would be much better pleased with the prospect of St Albans, which is not very famous for seeing far'.

At Heidelberg, where Churchill and the infantry caught up with the rest, Marlborough, says his chaplain, expressed concern for them. 'He was very sensible of the hardships the cavalry had endured by so many hard marches and . . . reflected on the sufferings of the Foot'. He accordingly ordered 'an early provision of shoes and other necessaries which would not be so easily found in an enemy's country'. Most of the infantry's shoes in the Blenheim tapestries are buckled and look more like boots. The cavalry, who in a charge rode knee to knee, wore protective thigh-boots or high, buttoned gaiters, the latter favoured by Marlborough himself.*

* The infantryman wore a tricorned hat, leather shoes, white or grey breeches with gaiters and a red coat embellished with linings and facings of varying hue according to regiment. He also wore cross-belts and carried a flintlock and bayonet, a sword,

On June 6th, after his advance guard had crossed the Neckar, Marlborough wrote to tell the Dutch that he was marching to the Danube. Except for stressing that he alone must be responsible, they took this surprisingly well.

The weather worsened. Owing to 'perpetual rains and badness of the road' the march from Eppingen to Lauffen took not one day, as planned, but two. Nor was the news good. Marlborough now knew for certain that Marsin had been reinforced by Tallard to the tune of 12,000 men. They were most of them raw recruits. But it was undeniable that on the one hand Tallard had shown brilliance and daring in smuggling that force through the Black Forest; and on the other, the Margrave of Baden had failed the allies by forbidding his men to try to intercept Tallard without him and had then arrived too late for action. If Marlborough was dismayed he never showed it. Riding resolutely at the head of his cavalry he now pressed on to Mundelsheim, where he was to meet Count Wratislaw and Prince Eugene.

*

On May 11th Marlborough had authorised George Stepney, our Ambassador in Vienna, to tell the Emperor Leopold and the Elector Palatine, in confidence, of his Danube plan; and on May 21st Leopold had agreed to send Prince Eugene to Germany. Lediard, one of the first to attempt a biography of Marlborough, went so far as to label him and Eugene as Twin-Constellations in Glory. Their consultations at Mundelsheim, he tells us, 'lasted several hours together; and the mutual satisfaction and opinion they conceived of each other's prudence and capacity must have been very great, since the reciprocal esteem they before had grew from thenceforward into so strict a friendship and confidence as

---

24 cartridges, a knapsack, cloak and cooking-pot, weighing in all about 50 pounds Officers carried swords and pistols, sergeants the half-pike or spontoon. Chandler: *Marlborough As Military Commander.*

very much contributed to the glorious successes which attended the arms of the allies during the whole war'. In short, at this first meeting the two commanders took to each other with a more than ordinary liking: greatness recognised greatness. 'Such harmony is in immortal souls'. In his speech and in his candour, though not in his swarthy looks, Eugene reminded Marlborough of his friend the Duke of Shrewsbury, nicknamed the King of Hearts.

Prince Eugene of Savoy, thirteen years younger than Marlborough, had been born in Paris and reared in the court of Louis XIV. His parents considered themselves ill-treated by the King who, for reasons of his own, decided that their son was better fitted for the Church than for the Army. In some respects - in Eugene's cold and ascetic outlook and in his lifelong celibacy - he may have been right; but the man was a born soldier none the less and one who, while still young, became the sworn enemy of France. His fame as a general spread after his conquest of the Turks. In the winter of 1703-4 the Emperor Leopold recalled him from Italy and made him President of the Council of War, in Vienna.

Marlborough knew, the instant he met him, that Providence had chosen the right man; and so in a climate of mutual trust secrets were exchanged. The moment came when Eugene felt he might touch upon the 'jealous temper and timid strategy' of the Margrave of Baden. The Emperor Leopold had been confided in and had given Eugene full powers to rid himself of the Margrave if the need arose. This secret news, gravely imparted, was gravely received.

But there were more cheerful moments. Lediard writes of a dinner 'as magnificent as the circumstances of time and place could admit of'; and certainly if the baggage-waggons had brought the larger pieces of Marlborough's plate still to be seen at Althorp - the wine-fountains and cisterns and pilgrim-bottles - the table, if not the food, must have been magnificent indeed; and we may be sure too that the wine was good.

33

After more talk it was decided that 'the two armies should join and that the Duke of Marlborough and Prince Louis of Baden should command each day, alternately, and that Prince Eugene should head a separate army on the Rhine'. For the time being at least, faces must be saved and immense tact shown. As a military historian has recently written, 'Throughout the war both sides found that fitting generals into the hierarchy in such a way that they fought the enemy rather than each other was as great a problem as finding the men for them to command and the money to provide for them'.* Allies, as Swift was to point out, can be mixed blessings; and while the French experienced this with the Elector of Bavaria, we had our troubles with, among others, the Emperor's Commander-in-Chief in Germany, the Margrave of Baden. As senior in command, Baden must have his day and be allowed to command on the Danube, although Marlborough would much have preferred Eugene, who now must be sent to the Rhine.

Marlborough, seeing again several moves ahead, remained impassive and, at his blandest, prepared to meet the Margrave at Gross Heppach. Before he arrived, however, the cavalry were reviewed by Eugene, who was impressed and said so in words which may have sounded better in French. 'Money,' he ended, 'which you don't want in England, will buy clothes and fine horses, but it cannot buy that lively air I see in every one of these troopers' faces'. Marlborough, who in youth had served under Turenne, rose to this occasion with the manners of Versailles. 'His Grace', says Hare, 'replied that that must be attributed to their heartiness for the public cause and the particular pleasure and satisfaction they had in seeing his Highness'.

Compliments and honours thickened the air. Wratislaw, on the part of the Emperor, offered Marlborough a prince-

* David Francis: *Marlborough's March to the Danube, 1704.* (Army Historical Research, Summer 1972)

dom of the Holy Roman Empire, a tempting present which, again with exquisite manners and expressions, had for the moment to be declined. When the Margrave of Baden joined them, all the motions of politeness were gone through again. In his official report Cardonnel noted: 'We joined the Prince of Baden two days ago and there seems to be a pretty good harmony between him and my Lord Duke'.

Marlborough's face, as we see it in Kneller's and Closterman's portraits, gives nothing away. It is all just so: the wig, the bland composure, the symmetry then so greatly admired. There is little hint of fire or indeed of expression. Yet again and again, as we read the records, we are amazed at his grasp and his mastery of detail. He was indeed, as Wellington said, remarkable for his clear, cool, steady understanding. At Gross Heppach, for example, the talks over, Eugene leaves for the Rhine, the Margrave for Bavaria. In Vienna the Emperor must cautiously be thanked about the princedom; in London Robert Harley congratulated on becoming Secretary of State ('I must very much depend on your good advice and directions'). The Dutch must be written to, spies listened to, letters and reports read and pondered, the Commissioner of the Bread instructed. 'I am very sensible', he tells his brother General Churchill, 'the Foot must have suffered by the great rains we have had, which I am afraid are not yet over . . . I would therefore have you manage your marches to Geislingen so as to give them the greatest ease'. And again: 'Pray acquaint Colonel Blood that he should spare the contractors' horses as much as may be and make use of as many others as the country can afford'. It was a hazardous business employing civilians to manage the artillery-waggons, for understandably, at the first sign or sound of the enemy they were apt to skedaddle and could then only be kept at their posts with musket or halberd.

Beyond Geislingen both the road and the weather worsened again and 'rain without intermission' fell on the artillery teams struggling and slithering their way through a narrow defile 'altogether impassable', as Hare noted, 'by any but such as were carried on by an invincible resolution'. Inevitably however some found it too much for them and for these a hospital was set up at Heidenheim. 'I desire you will forthwith send them thither in carts', wrote Marlborough to his brother on June 22nd, 'with an able chirurgeon and a maoseet two to look after them and . . . money for their subsn foite. We have this day', he adds, 'joined Prince Louis [Brac den] and shall not march far till you come up with us, which I pray may be as soon as conveniently you can . . . I long to have you with me, being your loving brother . . .'

Money for subsistence, not only for the sick but for all the troops, had been a mounting worry for Marlborough's secretary, Cardonnel, since the beginning of June. 'My Lord Treasurer', he reminds Paymaster Sweet in Holland, 'did positively promise that there should constantly be a month's advance for the whole army'. Yet here they were, nearing Bavaria, with precariously empty pockets. A private's pay, in all conscience, was little enough, (nominally eightpence a day, it seldom, with deductions for subsistence, came to more than fourpence), but for morale, if not for his very existence, that mite he must have; 'it being of the greatest consequence in the world', as Cardonnel put it, 'that the troops should not want . . . I wish to God,' he added, 'our campaign in these parts was over, for I fear we shall have great difficulties to struggle with'. Sweet, he complains, ignores his urgent letters and keeps him so much in the dark that he might just as well be in Constantinople . . . and so on. 'Bread', he says, 'we shall pay for in Holland, but I don't find you have yet remitted anything for our hospitals'.

What, then, of Marlborough's efficiency? What of his famous attention to detail? Is the whole operation to break down for want of cash? Paymaster Sweet may be led to believe it, for he is being too slow. But there are reserves, there are more reliable channels. Two brilliant officers, Lord Cutts (the Salamander) and Lieutenant-General Ingoldsby, long delayed at Harwich, are now on their way. On June 22nd Cardonnel writes from Launsheim to Ingoldsby:

... We are like to be in straits for want of money to subsist our troops and therefore I send you enclosed a letter of credit on Messrs Behagel & Neufville for 40,000 crowns, which you will please to bring with you in ducats, French pistols or French crowns. It will be a very great relief to us, for though I have sent to Nuremburg for money, yet I am confident they will not have cash enough to supply us; besides, we shall still have occasion for this sum. If Behagel & Neufville can't give you the whole sum, pray bring with you all you can get, the more the more welcome. Mr Fauconbridge at Mr Davenant's, I believe, will furnish you with a good waggon and horses to bring the money, but pray don't let it be over-loaden with other things . . .

By the same messenger he sends a letter to Lord Cutts:

I heartily congratulate with your Lordship upon your safe arrival upon this side after waiting so long at Harwich for a passage, and I hope you may still [manage to] be with us before we come to any manner of action. This we may almost reckon the first day of our campaign. Hitherto we have marched with our English Horse alone, which has been little more than easy travelling a country journey; but this afternoon the Dutch, Hanoverians and Hessians are come to the same ground with us, within a league of Prince Louis' army, which we shall join tomorrow, but believe shall not advance far till our Foot and artillery that are still four days behind join us, so that as I reckon this may go near to find you arrived at Frankfurt, if you hasten on to Nuremburg you may possibly be with us before we undertake anything.

Thanks to Ingoldsby and good staff-work, the cash arrived in time; but Sweet was not quickly forgiven. 'I can assure you', Cardonnel told him, 'the army had been near starving . . . I aim at nothing else than the good and preservation of the troops and take God to witness 'tis not one brass farthing advantage to me whencesoever the money comes'. One stands amazed at the man's industry. Letters and directions in English and in French pour out of Cardonnel's office – and what an office it is! 'I can't come at my documents once in a week', he tells Sweet, 'and then it may be in half an hour's time we must be packing up again'. And on top of all that there is what he calls 'our newspaper', which is something between a log and a news-sheet for the troops. On June 29th, for example, it sets it on record that 'General Churchill with the Foot and the Artillery joined the Army and took their post in the Lines where an interval was left for them. My lord Duke of Marlborough reviewed them as they came into camp'. 'And', Hare adds, 'found them very hearty and in good order after all their tedious marches . . . Only the Danish Horse are missing'.

By fortuitous contrast, on the very same day Marshal Tallard, writing to Louis XIV, calls his own army mediocre. The infantry, he admits, are tolerably good, but how can one conduct a campaign with only thirty-eight squadrons of cavalry and twelve of dragoons? Suppose the allies were to swoop down on him with a force twice as big as his own? Yes of course he must link up as quickly as possible with the Elector of Bavaria and his troops; but nothing is easy – even the Elector's letters take ten days to arrive.

Tallard, Count and Marshal of France, had in 1700 been Louis XIV's Ambassador at the Court of St James's. Though Saint-Simon is scathing about his diplomacy, he was popular in London and made many good friends, while at the same time warning Louis against measures which led to the Grand Alliance. In September 1701, when Louis assured James II on his deathbed that he would proclaim his son,

the Pretender, the rightful King of England, William III
dismissed Tallard, who returned to France and so to the
army. Historians have found him intelligent but wanting in
firmness. 'His training as a diplomat', says Trevelyan, 'made
him dread an open quarrel and seek always for a compromise.
But in war . . . one must fight or one must avoid a battle;
half measures are impossible'.

For Marlborough's men the most dangerous part of their
march was over and with the perils of the Rhineland behind
them they made for the Danube, with safer lines of communication running from the financial base at Frankfurt
down the Main towards Nuremburg and Nördlingen. In
little over five weeks the army had marched more than
250 miles. When the Danes and the Prussians had joined
them their strength rose to 40,000. On June 22nd they were
further reinforced at Launsheim by Baden's Imperialists.

The dusty caterpillar now dragged its slow length along
the Danube towards Donauwörth, the key town at the gate
of Bavaria. In his journal Hare has this entry:

> His Grace had no sooner come to his quarters than he was
> informed by a peasant living near Donauwörth that some
> 13,000 of the enemy were encamped upon the Schellen-
> berg. They were very busy in fortifying and entrenching
> themselves. Hereupon his Grace sent out the Quarter-
> master-General [Cadogan] with a party of 400 Horse to
> gain more particular intelligence . . . He resolved to
> attack.

3

The Schellenberg

The march concludes, the various realms are past,
Th' immortal Schellenberg appears at last:
Like hills th'aspiring ramparts rise on high,
Like valleys at their feet the trenches lie.
Batt'ries on batt'ries guard each fatal pass,
Threat'ning destruction; rows of hollow brass,
Tube behind tube, the dreadful entrance keep,
While in their wombs ten thousand thunders sleep.
Great Churchill owns, charm'd with the glorious sight,
His march o'erpaid by such a promis'd fight.

ADDISON, *The Campaign*

Of the long and noble range of tapestries 'dictated' by
Marlborough and woven in Brussels for his English palace,
none is more detailed than that headed DUNAWERT,
which shows the start of the operation known as the storming of the Schellenberg, the fortified hill guarding the town.

In the foreground Marlborough, on his charger, instructs
an officer who is almost certainly his Irish Quarter-Master
General Cadogan, while one of a picked team of running-
footmen, in fringed tunic and jockey-cap (his long hair tied
with ribbon), grasps his staff and listens as though poised
to pass the message on. Behind this group the village of
Berg is in flames; to the left of it the walled and river-
encircled town of Donauwörth nestles south-west of the
Schellenberg hill; and towards that hill, moving eastward
across the wide valley from Marlborough's vantage-point,
columns of dragoons ride with fascines* slung across their
saddle-pommels. At the foot of the hill the fascines are
dropped and piled so that the infantry, already drawn up in

* Fascine: a long cylindrical faggot of brushwood or the like, firmly bound together,
used in filling up ditches, constructing batteries etc. O.E.D.

battle-order about their standards, may help themselves
and so, when the attack is sounded, advance, using these
faggots for bridging the enemy's entrenchments.

Marlborough had three weeks before decided that to safe-
guard his supplies in Bavaria he would need to take Donauwörth and make it 'a magazine for the army'. And now, the
nearer he approached the more obvious it became that the
time to attack was now. Looking through his perspective-
glass at the Schellenberg, Marlborough, says Hare, 'plainly
perceived the enemy's posture upon it and that they made
two fronts, as if they expected to be attacked in two different
places. And besides, on the other side Donauwörth, beyond
the Danube, he saw that another camp was marked out,
with tents already pitched on each wing but none in the
centre. His Grace soon discovered them to be some cavalry,
arrived from the Elector's camp between Lauingen and
Dillingen, which had not yet passed the Danube, and did not
doubt but that there was infantry also coming from thence
to take their places in the centre'.

But what made for even more urgency was the state of the
enemy's defences which, in spite of desperate efforts on the
part of the Bavarian commander, Count d'Arco, and his
10,000 men, were still unfinished. On the heights of the
Schellenberg earthworks survived from the time when
Gustavus Adolphus had attacked it in 1632; and had there
been time now, they could have been extended to make a
naturally strong position impregnable. As it was, thick
woods on the east and north-east gave admirable cover,
while west and south were protected by the gradient and,
towards Donauwörth, by a small ruined fort and a covered
way. Batteries of cannon were in the wood and in the fort
as well as in the walls of the town itself.

The scene in the tapestry, recorded stitch by stitch, shows
the scene as Marlborough saw it on the afternoon of the
engagement, July 2nd; but detailed plans had been made
with the Margrave of Baden the day before. As the Mar-

grave, an old and cautious campaigner, must have realised, the situation, by all the rules of war he knew, called for a siege with heavy guns which, with luck, might batter the place to bits in a matter of weeks. This of course was out of the question. Yet Marlborough was convinced that, as Trevelyan put it, unless he stood upon the conquered summit of the Schellenberg before night fell, it would never be taken at all, and he would never set foot on the southern shore of the Danube. For next day Prince Louis would be most unlikely to take the responsibility of attacking. But there was also that prince's known lust for glory. Very well, the British and Dutch would lead the attack, taking the brunt, as a decoy to lure the enemy from his southern flank where, when the moment arrived, Baden and his Imperialists could rush straight in to victory.

From each battalion of his own army Marlborough chose one hundred and thirty men: storm troops totalling in all more than 6,000; to which the Margrave added three battalions of Imperial Grenadiers.* Pioneers for road-making and bridge-making went with them as at 3 a.m. they set out on a fifteen-mile march along appalling roads; while to head the assault when they got there, Peterborough's son Lord Mordaunt marched with a forlorn hope of fifty grenadiers.

Marlborough himself, writing later to Secretary Harley, gave the bare facts:

> ... Yesterday about three in the morning I marched with a detachment of 6,000 Foot, thirty squadrons of Horse and three regiments of Imperial grenadiers, leaving the whole army to follow; but the march being long and the roads very difficult, I could not reach the river Wernitz till about noon. We immediately used all the diligence we could in laying over the bridges, which being finished about three o'clock, the troops with the artillery marched over and,

* The Allies' forces at the Schellenberg totalled 25,000.

An English infantry-man with sword and flintlock

Overleaf. Fascine gatherers and dragoons

26TH FOOT.
CAMERONIANS

24TH FOOT.
SOUTH WALES
BORDERERS.

OFFICER
DANISH
CUIRASSIERS

1ST FOOT GUARDS
GRENADIER
GUARDS.

21ST FOOT
ROYAL SCOTS
FUSILIERS

16TH FOOT.
BEDFORDSHIRE
&
HERTFORDSHIRE
REGT.

Soldiers of Marlborough's army in the uniforms of 1704

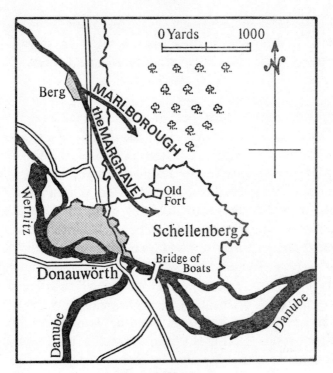

The Schellenberg

all things being ready, the attack began about six. We found the enemy very strongly entrenched and they defended themselves with great obstinacy for an hour and a half, during which there was a continued fire without any intermission . . .

Hare gives about four in the afternoon as the time of the troops' arrival at the foot of the Schellenberg. There, he adds, the infantry halted to receive the fascines from the dragoons, 'the enemy's cannon playing upon them from their batteries all the while'. In the meantime however, under cover of smoke screening the burning village of Berg, north of Donauwörth, Colonel Blood managed to plant cannon: a battery which, adds Hare, 'did good service'.

On a narrow front the lines of battle were formed: the

6,000 picked men in three ranks, supported by eight battalions of infantry, with a further eight in reserve, and thirty-five squadrons of cavalry close behind them.

*

Soon after six the drums beat and Lieutenant-General Goor, the Dutch general commanding the assault, led his detachment in six lines (four of infantry, two of cavalry) up the steep green slope, with the English, headed by Lord Mordaunt and his grenadiers, on their left, skirting the dense wood. Brigadier Ferguson told his men, as did the other officers, that the fascines were to be hurled into the enemy's entrenchments. Until that had been done, not a musket-shot could be fired. The advance was slow, the enemy's cannonade in the death-angle between fort and wood, murderous and relentless. Of Mordaunt's forlorn hope of fifty, only himself and ten others were not killed or wounded; while the leading troops in Ingoldsby's, Orkney's and Meredith's regiments were mown down by scores.

'However', says Hare, 'the Foot still advanced with great calmness and resolution to within eighty paces of the entrenchments, the Horse and Dragoons sustaining them as gallantly; Lieutenant-General Lumley keeping close with eighteen squadrons in the first line and Lieutenant-General Hompesch bringing up the other seventeen in the second. The enemy, expecting the attack, ceased firing with great shot and upon the nearer approach of our lines loaded their cannon with case-shot,* which they poured in amongst our men, doing very great execution'.

Marlborough afterwards described the action as 'the warmest that has been known for many years . . . The battalion of Guards, one of my Lord Orkney's regiments, and Ingoldsby's, were those that suffered most'. His friend General Goor was killed in the first onslaught. As other officers fell there was a check and some confusion; then a

* Case-shot: a collection of small projectiles put up in cases to fire from a cannon.

rally while, as Hare says, 'our men pursued the attack and bore the enemy's fire with incredible bravery'. And then - the kind of mistake that can cost a victory - 'our men being advanced as far as the hollow way which ran before the enemy's entrenchments, threw down their fascines and so quite lost the advantage of them'. They then stood and faced a fusillade while some of the Bavarians rushed out with bayonets. To withstand that called for heroism and found it in the Guards who, with most of their officers killed or wounded, refused to yield an inch.

When at last the dismounted dragoons of the Scots Greys, led by Lord John Hay, reached level ground they broke into a charge and rushed at full speed, yelling at the top of their lungs as they cleared the outworks and made for the parapet. For those lining that parapet it was, says de la Colonie, who was one of them, 'truly alarming. I ordered our drums', he remembers, 'to beat the charge to drown the noise lest it have a bad effect upon our people . . . the shouts and yells might have caused a general panic'. No doubt they were meant to.

We were all fighting hand to hand, hurling them back as they clutched at the parapet. Men were slaying or tearing at the muzzles of guns and the bayonets which pierced their entrails, crushing under their feet their own wounded comrades and even gouging out their opponents' eyes with their nails when the grip was so close that neither could make use of their weapons. I verily believe that it would have been quite impossible to find a more terrible representation of Hell itself than was shown in the savagery of both sides on this occasion.

Then came a brief lull when the enemy thought they had won the day. The parapet was heaped with dead and dying, while most of the rest were invisible, having fallen back into a dip in the slope, which just there was so steep that from the parapet only the tops of our standards could be seen. Generals dismounted and rallied their shattered regiments, before leading them forward, sword in hand. The German General Styrum was mortally wounded. English, Scots, Dutch, Hanoverians, Hessians and the rest died where they fell by the hundred in the death-angle; but Lumley and his cavalry charged another sortie of the Bavarians and drove them back.

If ever our troops needed and deserved a stroke of luck it was now and they had it. While near the parapet the air was still thick with grenades, a lieutenant with twenty men was sent to the covered way on the south-west slope, which he expected to find bristling with men and muskets, if not with mortars and mines. 'This officer', says de la Colonie, 'who fully believed he had received his sentence of death, was agreeably surprised to find the *glacis* deserted . . . The town commandant, upon whom d'Arco had relied so much, instead of lining his covered way with his best troops, had withdrawn them all into the main works . . . shut up his troops and locked the gates and the result was our ruin'. It may have been so. At the same time one needs to remember that the withdrawal of enemy troops from that flank, to help withstand the main attack in the centre, had probably all along been Marlborough's aim.

'When they found themselves safe from attack on the south side', de la Colonie goes on, 'they hastened to make the most of the daylight left to them. It was nearly seven when they began their movement to turn this flank, which they did without making any change in their order of battle. They had merely to turn their column to the flank and by reason of the fall of the ground succeeded in changing their position to their right, near the *glacis*, without meeting any obstacle or being seen by us . . . We never believed it possible that they would approach from this direction'. When he did spot some of our men - or they may have been Imperialists, who were now joining us - he thought they must be French reinforcements. 'I became aware', he says, 'of several lines

of infantry on our left flank in greyish white uniforms*
and . . . shouted to my men that they were Frenchmen'. As
they came closer however he noticed bunches of straw and
leaves attached to their standards – 'badges they are accus-
tomed to wear for battle†; and at that very moment I was
struck by a ball in the right lower jaw . . . the front of my
jacket deluged with blood . . . I shouted as loudly as I could
that no one was to quit the ranks and then formed my men
in column along the entrenchments facing the wood'.

From the allies' point of view what had been a heroic
shambles now began to look more like an orderly exercise.
No longer at the mercy of the cannon-filled woods on their
left, no longer in the death-angle between that battery and
the answering one in the old fort, they could now form
four-deep on a wider front before steadily advancing with
bayonets to occupy those half-empty entrenchments. Even
so they still met with stubborn resistance and were now
within range of cannon mounted on or within the walls of
Donauwörth.

In this dangerous situation the Margrave of Baden and his
infantry played vigorous parts, winning the trenches and
then again attacking on the flank, to let the Dutch and the
English through. 'But for all that', says Hare, 'the enemy
still continued to oppose their entrance and disputed it so
obstinately that Lieutenant-General Lumley ordered Lord
John Hay's regiment of dragoons, who had re-mounted, to
dismount and charge the enemy on foot. This order was
forthwith obeyed by that noble Lord, who dismounted and
put himself at the head of his regiment and was marching
up bravely to attack on foot just as the enemy began to give
way and our men had entered the trenches. Hereupon he

* White was the Bourbon colour, but the undyed wool of the French 'white-coats'
made them greyish white.

† The wear and tear of campaign often caused the badly-fixed colours of uniforms to
run or fade, and much use was made by the Allies of green branches or bundles of straw
worn in the hat for recognition. The French similarly used white rosettes. Chandler:
Marlborough As Military Commander. This is plainly seen in Laguerre's frescoes in Marlborough House.

47

remounted and soon got over with our other squadrons, which now put the enemy to flight and pursuing them killed a great many, took thirteen of their colours and drove great numbers of them into the Danube'.

Their commander Count d'Arco escaped across the Danube to Donauwörth, before the rest of the fugitives swarmed on and sank the bridge of boats. His plate, though doubtless not to be compared with Marlborough's, made part of the booty which included 'all their tents standing and sixteen brass field-pieces'.

From the top of the Schellenberg, an oval plateau half a mile across, Marlborough, having reached it with the cavalry and ordered the pursuit, looked down on a scene very different from the one he had first viewed fifteen miles off on the other side of the valley. Trevelyan brilliantly describes it:

It was near sunset, but there was light enough to see beyond the Danube the vast open plains deep in standing corn and circled with dark forests, those southern plains which the capture of Donauwörth would open to his advance. To the south-east lay the straight, wooded line of the Lech, marking the boundary of Bavaria, now at his mercy. At his feet stretched the broad, silver ribbon of the Danube, which he had come so far to find, henceforth forever associated with his name. The bridge of boats, which d'Arco had laid across it below the town, was breaking up beneath the wait of madly struggling fugitives; many had crossed; many were drowning in the river or trying to steer the drifting boats; many who had been cut off on the northern shore could be seen running for their lives among the reed-beds or the corn, vainly endeavouring to avoid the rise and fall of the sabres of the red-coated horsemen. Looking to the east Marlborough could see another dark mass of fugitives near the village of Zirgesheim, straining to escape from the pursuing squadrons into the wooded hills beyond. Only to the west he could detect a few battalions who had found their way into the streets of Donauwörth, crossing the Danube by the town bridge in tolerable order. Then darkness fell and the scene was blotted out. And with the darkness sheets of rain descended in pitiless brutality on the maimed and dying men, gathered from all the four corners of Europe to perish together on that tragic hill.*

Donauwörth, now all but defenceless, surrendered. The cost had been heavy. The allies had lost eight generals and twenty-eight brigadiers and colonels; their casualties totalling 5,340; although as Mr Chandler points out, had Marlborough listened to Baden and postponed the attack, the death-roll might have been far longer. The Bavarians and the French lost 5,000 men. In Goor Marlborough lost not only a good general but a helpful friend. Among English officers wounded were another of his personal friends, Colonel Meredith, Colonel Palmer and Major-General Wood. The Margrave of Baden had been slightly wounded, as too had the hereditary Prince of Hesse. Cadogan had had his horse shot under him, but had escaped unhurt.

The last order Marlborough had given before the attack was to Hudson, the Commissioner of the Hospital, to march day and night to Nördlingen, where he was to establish a larger hospital than that set up en route at Heidenheim, where 1,200 sick had been left behind. After the storming of the Schellenberg Marlborough, Hare tells us, ordered the wounded to be 'dressed with all possible haste and forthwith sent to the hospitals'. For this purpose the sprung, two-wheeled cart he had designed must have come in useful; though even then the suffering scarcely bears thinking of. Arrived at Nördlingen, twelve miles from Donauwörth (it meant crossing the Wernitz), what was to be expected? Of course no antiseptics and no anaesthetics.

* G. M. Trevelyan: *England Under Queen Anne*. Volume I: *Blenheim* (Longmans).

With a not hopelessly damaged limb one might find oneself in a queue for amputation by someone better qualified for carpentry than for anything else. With serious internal injuries one's doom was sealed. Responsible for all military hospitals was Dr Thomas Lawrence, Physician-General and First Physician to Queen Anne. Officially too he was Marlborough's doctor and was present at Blenheim. The man in charge of the hospital at Nördlingen, however, was Hudson, not a doctor, not named in history books, but nevertheless dependable and kind. The first helpful thing he did was to have the hospital, such as it was, ready in time to receive the Schellenberg wounded. He then, with assistance, patched them up as best he could and, often thanks to tough constitutions, sent back the relatively lucky ones to their regiments.

'All his Grace's care was now employed', notes Hare, 'about sending the wounded away to the hospital; and as there was a particular Hand of Providence directed him in all his marches and designs, so it was very remarkable in the happy arrival of the apothecaries, surgeons and medicaments at Nördlingen in the time of the action and that they had notice to make their preparations by the noise of the engagement, which was about twelve miles from them'.

Cardonnel, writing from Obermergen to Teale, the apothecary at Nördlingen, tells him: 'His Grace has given orders that all the widows in the army should repair to you to serve as nurses, and must have some small subsistence allowed them; though there should be more than you should have occasion for as nurses. His Grace would have an account of their numbers and which of them are desirous to go for England. If you can spare them, they shall have passes and money . . .' It sounds a sensible idea, if only as occupational therapy for the widows; but one would like to hear more of their nursing. So little has been said of wives (Hare never mentions them); yet now of a sudden we hear of so many widows that there may be too many to act as nurses.

As for the particular hand of Providence, this of course is to be expected from a chaplain on his way to becoming a bishop. But Marlborough too, writing to Queen Anne from Donauwörth, assures her: 'Our success is in a great measure owing to the particular blessing of God and on the unparalleled courage of your troops. I shall endeavour to improve', he adds, 'upon this happy beginning, to your Majesty's glory and to the benefit of all'. The following Sunday was to be solemnly observed as a day of thanksgiving, 'as well to return thanks for this success as of prayers for imploring the continuance of it to the armies of the allies'. Prayers then ascended for the English and the Dutch, the Austrians, Hanoverians, Hessians and Prussians, the Danes and the Scots, but not of course for the French and the Bavarians, nor for the Irish known as the Wild Geese, who were in French pay.

Blackader too had solemn business. 'In the evening', he wrote in his journal, 'I went alone into the field of battle and there got a preaching from the dead. The carcases were very thick strewed upon the ground, naked and corrupting. Yet all this works no impression or reformation upon us, seeing the bodies of our comrades and friends lying as dung upon the face of the earth. Lord, make me humble and thankful. I trusted in Thee that I should set up many Ebenezers through Germany, and here in the field of the slain do I set up my memorial: Hitherto Thou hast helped me'. He then left for Nördlingen, there to comfort the dying and administer the last rites.

In 1705 General de Blainville, visiting the Schellenberg, found vast quantities of skulls and bones there and, on a heap of rags, an English grenadier's cap (the tall kind, more practical than the tricorne when it came to hurling grenades), upon which Queen Anne's motto SEMPER EADEM (always the same) was still legible. For the nurses at Nördlingen however and for a great many more the world had changed and the case was altered.

4

Bavaria Burns

With fire and sword the country round
Was wasted far and wide,
And many a childing mother then
And new-born baby died;
But things like that, you know, must be
At every famous victory.
                    SOUTHEY, *After Blenheim*

Max Emanuel, Elector of Bavaria, arrived too late to save the
Schellenberg and too late for the burning of Donauwörth,
which he had ordered. The inhabitants put out what fire
there was and threw open their gates, while the Elector
retired to Augsburg, a strongly fortified city on the west
bank of the river Lech. At the same time he sent urgently to
Villeroi for reinforcements, convinced as he was that the
French troops already with him, under Marsin, were not
enough.

What Hare calls the wooing of the Elector, to persuade
him to defect to the allies, now became something very
much fiercer than a gentle courtship. Four hundred horsemen, the Chaplain-General goes on to say, were commanded to burn and destroy the countryside 'within sight
of the Elector, to try whether this would have any better
effect upon him. But neither this nor the pressing instances
of his Electress, who was with child, the advice of his
ministers, nor the doleful representations of his subjects
could move him and therefore it was evident that the allies
must go on with fire and sword, since there was no other
way left to bring him to reason'.

The Elector was desperate. Tough though he was, reports
of the Schellenberg massacre had made him weep. Now he

was between two fires: Marlborough and Wratislaw on the one hand, offering bribes to join them, with the alternative of Bavaria's devastation; and on the other, Marsin and his staff, who threatened the withdrawal of all French troops should the Elector dare to meet Wratislaw for negotiation. Even so, the Electress's pleas for her adopted country (she was Polish) had all but won him over when the smuggled news came through that Tallard and 36,000 men were on their way. This tipped the balance. The Elector, in Sir Winston's phrase, 'decided that Bavaria must burn', as indeed a large number* of villages did, while Tallard's army marched from Ulm.

On this question of the laying waste of Bavaria, even Sir Winston has qualms about his ancestor's attitude. After quoting Marlborough's letters to his wife – 'You will, I hope, believe me that my nature suffers when I see so many fine places burnt'; and 'This is so contrary to my nature that nothing but absolute necessity could have obliged me to consent to it' – he tersely adds: 'But there is not much in all this. Men in power must be judged not by what they feel but by what they do. To lament miseries which the will has caused is a cheap salve to a wounded conscience'. He does admit however that 'its military usefulness cannot be disputed', a view which would certainly have been endorsed by Cadogan who, as early as May 30th, had written: ' 'tis absolutely necessary to hasten putting in execution the project of reducing the Elector of Bavaria before he can receive a greater succour'.

After their victory at the Schellenberg Marlborough and the Margrave might still have been cut off from Eugene and from their supplies had Tallard and the Elector combined to march between them. Luckily for us this proved beyond them. In the meantime however neither Augsburg

---

* 'Marlborough burned not less than 120 villages' (Belloc). Captain Parker writes of '372 towns, villages and farmhouses laid in ashes'. Other writers put the number of villages burned as high as 400.

nor Munich could be attacked without a siege-train, and even the siege of the small market-town called Rain (July 10-16), without adequate artillery, took several days. Nor were things improved by the Margrave who, nursing a wounded toe, complained to the Emperor of his allies' incendiarism and began to talk of besieging Ingoldstadt, the enemy's last stronghold on the Danube between Vienna and Dillingen.

At this time Marlborough, while still in the midst of his army, must have been feeling much alone. Goor was dead, Goor the Dutch general who, as he told Sarah, 'helped me in a great many things which I am now forced to do myself'. Cadogan and Cardonnel could always be relied on; but one wonders if any of them found time to sleep. 'Our greatest difficulty', Marlborough wrote to Godolphin on July 6th, 'is that of making our bread follow us; for the troops that I have the honour to command cannot subsist without it, and the Germans that are used to starve cannot advance without us'. Three days later he told his wife: 'I am extremely pleased to know that I have it now in my power that the poor soldiers shall not want bread'.* Brigadier Baldwin was instructed 'to get up all the corn he could and put into the magazines [granaries] at Neuberg, making a distinction between that corn which belonged to the inhabitants of that place and what belonged to the subjects of the Elector of Bavaria. He was further commanded', Hare adds, 'to send some cattle forthwith to the hospital at Nördlingen, to be distributed among the sick and wounded . . . and to gather up all the carriages and horses he could to bring ammunition'.

Crops were heavy but, not surprisingly, the reapers were few, most of the villagers having run away. The corn, says Hare, 'now began to shed as it stood and whole fields were

---

* Armies could march and fight over the distance they could carry their bread, habitually halting every fourth day to set up field ovens and bake a further supply . . . Marlborough was outstandingly successful at most aspects of field administration. Chandler: *Marlborough As Military Commander.*

thereby spoiled and lost. The cavalry had no great occasion
for it, because they had plenty of oats and very good hay
from the meadows lying near the rivulets which everywhere
abound in this country'; but the horses had riders and the
riders needed bread. At Aicha, a small town whose gates
were reluctantly opened, there were watermills 'very much
damaged'. Marlborough gave orders for their instant repair.
The great brewery too at Aicha was found to have been
sabotaged; whereupon 'His Grace commanded the inhabitants to repair it and to set all their brewhouse to work
forthwith for the supplying the sutlers of both wings of the
army with beer'. So much for bread, so much for beer; and
now those officers who had been held up at Harwich -
Cutts, Ingoldsby and Webb - arrived from Frankfurt 'with
a considerable sum of money for the use of the army'. It
almost called for a *feu de joie*.

On July 21st Hare noted: 'It was with great reluctance
that his Grace saw all the country on fire about him and
therefore he ordered a stop to be put to it in hopes that the
peasants would return to the villages that were yet standing
and reap the corn'. He gave orders too to spare the woods,
'stately and numerous', most of them consisting of fir
trees. Bavaria had not, as some said, been reduced to ashes.
De la Colonie found the damage 'as nothing compared with
the reports current through the country'.

Much of Cardonnel's correspondence was now with
hospitals. It had been found that most of those 1,200
infantrymen who had fallen out and been sent to Heidenheim were 'half-foundered by the long march, so that they
wanted rest rather than physic'; while to Hudson at Nördlingen he wrote:

Here are some gentlemen come to complain of their being
overburthened in the villages in your neighbourhood
with the wounded soldiers. I comprehend little of the
matter, but in general I think it is that the town, to save

themselves, would throw all the burthen upon the villages. All I have in command from his Grace is that you endeavour to give everybody the best satisfaction and to make them all as easy as you can...Brigadier Baldwin will send you about twenty cows or oxen for the use of the wounded men. His Grace would have them distributed to the troops in English and Dutch pay. I need not tell you charity begins at home . . .

All that could be done for the men was done, but for Marlborough himself this waiting time, with crisis imminent, made for what he mildly called uneasiness. 'Uncertainty', he once wrote, 'is the worst of all conditions, for death itself is easier than the fear of it'. In this daunting dilemma Sir Winston sees him 'in the flicker of that baleful sunlight which was to play at Moscow upon Napoleon, who also sought a treaty or a battle at the end of a long march far from home'. None knew better than Marlborough that in this, perhaps the greatest gamble in history, he could not afford to lose. The Emperor, the Dutch, the Germans, all the confederates counted on him, while at the same time reminding him that the responsibility was his. At home his political enemies blamed him for putting the army at risk and bayed for his blood.

Tallard, as everyone imagined, was by forced marches steadily making his way, with 36,000 men, through the Black Forest. He had indeed been warned that should time be lost, the Elector might change sides; but Providence, now and a little later, was not on Tallard's side. After a delay of nearly three weeks while he awaited Louis XIV's sanction for his march, he met with an absurd mishap: 300,000 rations for his troops were found to be uneatable. For emergency supplies it meant halting and waiting. Tallard then decided to besiege Villingen. This at least would protect his line of supply and might, as he hoped, compel Eugene to stay near the Rhine. Tallard had had no news of the Schellenberg. Marsin's first cry for help had failed to reach him and when the second one did, Tallard still took time to abandon the siege, while his troops continued to plunder the countryside. Many of them were murdered. But the threat of starvation was a real one. The harvest, Tallard told Versailles, was abundant, but it would take time 'pour en rassembler les fruits'; and time was what, besides food and money, he was short of. There was too a serious outbreak of glanders or 'German sickness' among the cavalryhorses. His muddles and misfortunes, in fact, throw Marlborough's competence into sharp relief.

In spite of all this, however, Tallard himself never seems to have gone without. 'The Marshal invited me in to share his breakfast chicken', the Comte de Mérode-Westerloo remembers, 'he was very partial to the fine martial air imparted by receiving from a page a chunk of cold meat or a smoked tongue merely wrapped in a napkin, with a hunk of bread. He would on occasion however entertain anything up to a hundred officers at a time, during the first or second halt of the day's march, keeping two mule trains laden with good things to eat – and wines too – at the head of the army for this very purpose'. His army, urged forward on short commons, reached Ulm on July 29th.

As for Eugene, while deploring the devastation in Bavaria and expressing doubts on other scores – 'If he has to go home without having achieved his objective', he wrote of Marlborough to the Duke of Savoy, 'he will certainly be ruined' – he never wavered in his support. As Sir Winston sees them, Eugene and Marlborough were two lobes of one brain, their every move pondered and synchronised. On July 18th, for example, while Tallard was bombarding Villingen, Eugene with 18,000 men left the Lines of Stollhofen and 'observed' Tallard from Rothweil. Villeroi's army was too near for Eugene to risk an attack; but if Tallard joined the Elector, Eugene would, by keeping pace with him, be ready to link up with Marlborough. As it was, he successfully contrived to 'amuse' the enemy and by marching twenty miles northward to Tübingen convinced Villeroi that, instead of heading for Marlborough and the Danube, Eugene aimed to return to the Rhine and the Lines of Stollhofen. But for this, Villeroi would have obeyed the command of his distant king and made for the Danube. 'Eugene knew', adds Sir Winston, 'that whatever might miscarry behind him on the Rhine or in Würtemberg, he must arrive on the Danube, somewhere between Ulm and Donauwörth, at the same time that Tallard joined the Elector. Marlborough in all his conduct counted upon him to do this, and his own arrangements made the junction sure and certain'.

A glance at Cardonnel's letters from Friedberg (near Augsburg) to Hudson at the Nördlingen hospital shows some of the smaller troubles he was now having to deal with: 'I fear this hot weather will not help us much. If there be any tricks played in the villages in your neighbourhood I am satisfied it must be by the foreigners and not our people. Brigadier Baldwin writ long since to my Lord Duke that he would send you twenty cows and I wonder he has not done it . . . Marshal Tallard is approaching . . .' To 'deprive the enemy as far as we can of any subsistence' the burning of Bavaria has been resumed; and this sickens Cardonnel as it does his commander. 'We have made no progress since our success at Schellenberg', he tells Matthew Prior, 'except that it be burning and destroying the Elector's country, wherein we have not been sparing; our last march was all fire and smoke. We are now going to besiege Ingoldstadt, and I wish to God it were well over that I might get safe out of this country'. His feelings no doubt were shared throughout the army. Ingoldstadt however was not Marlborough's objective but Baden's.

The Margrave of Baden, says Kane,* was an old, captious general, not for running hazards. In action at the Schellen-

* Brigadier-General Richard Kane: *The Wars of William III and Queen Anne* (1735).

Donauworth from the Schellenberg

Overleaf. The Action at the Schellenberg.
Marlborough with Cadogan and one of the running footmen by whom
he sent out his orders and received information during the battle

The Margrave of Baden

The Elector of Bavaria

berg he had been dashing and courageous; so much so that the Dutch had struck a medal, giving him all the credit. Since then however his pro-Bavaria carpings had made Marlborough suspicious and these doubts had been doubled by those of Eugene. Furthermore, the Margrave had broken his promise to supply 40 large cannon and 100 bread-waggons. 'On our second day's march', Kane remembers, 'just as we were pitching our camp, Prince Eugene . . . came riding along our Line and went to the Duke's quarters, where they settled the operations of the campaign and formed a scheme for sending the Prince of Baden out of their way'. But it was in fact more subtle than that. On July 31st Marlborough had written to Eugene to tell him the Margrave was bent on besieging Ingoldstadt 'with the troops we have here, without any reinforcements from your side'. Marlborough was in favour of letting him go, even at the cost of 15,000 men, but most of those troops, he suggested – Prussian, Danes and Imperialists – should be Eugene's. Eugene, Marlborough further suggested, should promote the idea as though it were his own, at the same time offering as an alternative that he himself should march and lay siege to Ingoldstadt, the one Danube stronghold left to the enemy between Dillingen and Vienna and a prize certain to reflect glory on whichever general won it. The stratagem worked. Baden agreed to go.

On August 5th Tallard and his 36,000 reached Augsburg, to join the Franco-Bavarian army at Biberbach the following day. In his report on the Elector's troops Tallard pronounced them excellent; but if only there were more of them! Only twenty-three squadrons and five battalions, he said, were then with the army, the rest being still dispersed throughout Bavaria to guard the Elector's estates.

Marlborough, moving north to Schrobenhausen and Sandizell, was within twenty miles of the enemy, while Eugene marched to Höchstädt, which had a small allied garrison in its castle. On the 6th Eugene rode over to see

Marlborough at Schrobenhausen, where plans for the siege of Ingoldstadt were completed with the Margrave. The whole of the following day was spent by Marlborough and Eugene with an escort, all on horseback, examining the countryside. And if, as has been said, an eye for country is essential to every successful commander, then both these generals most certainly had it. Both had been trained in France; and as for Marlborough, as Uncle Toby reminded Corporal Trim, he could never have reached the Danube without 'Geography'.*

On August 9th the Margrave and his 15,000 left for Ingoldstadt while Eugene returned to Höchstädt and Marlborough made a five-mile march to Exheim. On August 10th Eugene sent an urgent despatch to Marlborough from Munster to tell him, 'The enemy have marched. It is almost certain that the whole army is crossing the Danube at Lauingen . . . The plain of Dillingen is crowded with troops. I have held on all day here, but with 18 battalions I dare not risk staying the night . . . Everything, milord, consists in speed and that you put yourself forthwith in movement to join me tomorrow, without which I fear it will be too late. In short, all the enemy is there, . . .'. But the Margrave was not recalled. This in itself, as Sir Winston points out, was a remarkable decision. Marlborough knew precisely how many troops the enemy had and how many he himself could count on when Eugene's army had combined with his own: two opposing hosts so nearly equal that, if battle were joined and things went badly, Baden's 15,000 might have made all the difference between defeat and victory. Yet the risk was taken. If what Marlborough called a fair occasion arose, a full-scale battle would have to be hazarded. It was a risk which Baden would almost certainly not have sanctioned; so he had to go.

And here again sharp contrast appears between staff conditions in the opposing armies. From the allied forces Marlborough and Eugene took care to rid themselves of

* Laurence Sterne: *Tristram Shandy*.

friction and all danger of it before the battle of Blenheim began; whereas in the Franco-Bavarian army Tallard, Marsin and the Elector found themselves in disagreement soon after they had joined forces, when the Elector wanted to attack Eugene at Höchstädt and Tallard demurred. Tallard, the diplomat was for compromise. Take no risks with the King's troops, he told Marsin, we have only to dodge Marlborough until the autumn, when we may safely withdraw into winter quarters. There was much to be said for it, perhaps everything; but the Elector had other views and Marsin supported him. In the matter of camps too they were divided. Having moved to the ground vacated by Eugene at Höchstädt and captured the small garrison there in the Schloss, Tallard was all for digging themselves in in that strong position, naturally protected as it was by the Danube and by a formidable marsh. But no, the Elector objected, there was no forage; they must march north to Lutzingen and make sure of it before the enemy took it. Marsin called Tallard aside: surely he could see sense in the Elector's suggestion? He could not; but as he sadly wrote afterwards, this was a classic case of the infallible rule for victory: never have more than one man in command of the army. In any war, in any battle one may count upon the enemy making mistakes. Where genius comes in is seeing to it that his errors are worse than one's own. At the battle of Blenheim Marlborough saw to it that on his side the part left to chance should be as small as man could make it.

Time and again too, throughout his campaigns, we find Marlborough scoring heavily for his secret service. Thrifty in some ways, with public money he bribed munificently and got good returns for it. Now, nearing the battlefield, he knew the strength of the enemy's forces: between fifty and sixty thousand, with an advantage over us in artillery. They had failed to discover ours. Not a word of Baden's march to Ingoldstadt had reached Tallard. On the contrary, thanks to 'deserters' strategically dangled by Marlborough and swiftly grabbed, Tallard was informed, not once but several times, that the Margrave and his men were still on the strength of the allied forces.

In the final camping ground on the wide plain between the wooded slopes of Lutzingen, on their left, and Blenheim, beside the Danube, on their right, Tallard put in a strong plea for a redoubt and for damming the Danube tributary called the Nebel. At this the Elector recoiled. 'I do hope', he said, 'you don't mean to start digging up earth'.

In the official list of equipment for Marlborough's army there are items described as instruments for removing earth. Could they have been spades?

II

BATTLE

5

Before the Battle

But now the trumpet terrible from far
In shriller clangours animates the war,
Confed'rate drums in fuller consort beat
And echoing hills the loud alarm repeat:
Gallia's proud standards, to Bavaria's join'd,
Unfurl their gilded lilies in the wind.

ADDISON, *The Campaign*

Eugene, falling back along the Danube from Höchstädt to the Kessel, near Donauwörth, was in a vulnerable position until Marlborough could join him. Reinforcements were sent. At midnight on August 9th Marlborough ordered the Duke of Wirtemberg to set out with twenty-eight squadrons of cavalry and to cross the Danube at Merxheim. Churchill, with twenty battalions of infantry and artillery, was to follow him; but the recent rains had swollen the rivers, and pontoon-bridges had laboriously to be made.

On the 10th Marlborough rode at the head of the main army, to camp that evening in the neighbourhood of Rain. From his quarters in the abbey of Nieder Schonfelt he wrote to his duchess, to the Margrave (promising to cover the siege of Ingoldstadt), to Harley and to Godolphin. 'I have this day', he told the Lord Treasurer, 'ordered twenty-eight squadrons and twenty battalions of Foot to pass the Danube for reinforcing Prince Eugene's army at Donauwörth and have given the necessary orders that I may follow with the whole army as soon as I shall be certain that the Elector and the Marshals have passed the Danube with their whole army . . . When Prince Eugene and I are joined our army will consist of 160 squadrons and 65 battalions . . . The French make their

65

boasts of having a great superiority, but I am very confident they will not venture a battle. Yet if we find a fair occasion we shall be glad to embrace it, being persuaded that the ill condition of our affairs in most parts requires it . . . I am afraid I shall be much put to it to get bread for the first ten days, notwithstanding the two hundred waggons I am obliged to keep, without which we could not march till we had our magazines first made'.

At eleven that night an express arrived from Eugene: the rest of the enemy's army had crossed the Danube. Wirtemberg had arrived and the Schellenberg was being prepared for defence, in case the Kessel line had to be abandoned. Marlborough sent off a messenger to his brother, ordering him to leave for Donauwörth at dawn.

The second line of infantry followed Churchill over the Danube, while Marlborough with the first line and the cavalry crossed the Lech at Rain and the Danube at Donauwörth. When the Wernitz too had been crossed, Marlborough drew up the cavalry on high ground, within sight of Eugene, and waited for Churchill and the infantry to join him. This they soon did and the whole force moved on to link up with Eugene at about six in the evening, between the Kessel and the Danube, the left being encamped at Munster. Colonel Blood with the artillery, having in eight hours marched twenty-four miles, joined the rest at dawn the next day.

*

A French General sent an account of the events, from Strasbourg, on August 30th to his Minister for War. Since he too fought in the battle his narrative is worth quoting:

The army marched, the twelfth [of August] . . . to go and encamp at Blenheim. The camp was hardly marking when information was brought to the Marshal that the

66

enemy appeared on the other side of the rivulet that bordered the front of our camp. He went that way immediately and having caused some troops to go over, the enemy retired to their camp.

Several people pressed the Elector to march up to them, assuring him that they were not joined [by the Margrave of Baden]. The Marshal dissuaded him from it, representing to him that before they advanced they ought to be thoroughly informed. In order to that, a great detachment was made to approach them nearer and we made some prisoners who assured us that they were joined; whereupon we returned back and had no other thoughts but to encamp.

On the morning before the battle, August 12th, Marlborough and Eugene with an escort rode to the village of Tapfheim where, from the church tower, they focused perspective-glasses on the plain of Höchstädt. Though at least five miles off, they were able, says Hare, to see

the whole army of the enemy in full march towards the same hill where their squadrons of cavalry were, and a camp there marking out. Hereupon his Grace took a view of all the avenues to the enemy, and finding a ravine or hollow way running parallel with the Kessel above the village of Tapfheim, about two miles from our camp, he gave orders that a body of pioneers should be immediately employed to level it; and having commanded the piquet-guard to draw up behind the ravine to cover the workmen, he returned with Prince Eugene to his quarters at Munster. Just as they were sitting down to dinner, intelligence was brought that the enemy's squadrons had attempted to fall upon our workmen, but had been repulsed by the guard which covered them; whereupon the generals immediately ordered their horses . . .

Lord Cutts and others, 'showing an eager desire to come to an engagement', rushed to help. On reaching the ravine however they found that the enemy had already retired. All then returned to camp except for Rowe's brigade and some Hessian infantry commanded by Major-General Wilkes, who spent the night in Tapfheim.

'Almost all the generals were against my Lord's attacking the enemy', wrote Hare the day after Blenheim, 'they thought it so difficult'; a statement endorsed by the Earl of Orkney, who played a leading part and owned afterwards that 'considering the ground where they were camped and the strength of their army', he too would have been against it. As at the Schellenberg, so at Blenheim: by all the rules of conventional warfare it was out of the question.

The battleground was a plain nearly six miles long, 'the entrance into it not being above the breadth of a cannon-shot', but soon widening to a breadth of about four miles. To the enemy's left the ground rose slightly and gradually to the dense woods bordering Lutzingen, where the Elector had his headquarters. To their right ran the Danube, deep and tortuous; their whole front being protected by marshes and streams, the chief of them, the Nebel, only twelve feet wide but having in places steep banks. The wide plain was dotted with villages, 'rendering', as Lediard says, 'the march of the confederate army to attack the enemy very trouble-some'. In the central part, on the Elector's right and on Tallard's left, lay Oberglau, where Marsin posted fourteen battalions under General de Blainville. Between Oberglau and Blenheim, on Tallard's right, General Zurlauben was in command of more than seventy squadrons of cavalry. At Tallard's rear were the villages of Sonderheim and Höch-städt, the hamlet after which the battle was at first named. Blenheim (locally Blindheim) was a village of some three hundred small houses or cottages, many of them thatched, standing about a furlong from the Danube and with its

68

farms clustered about a church and high-walled church-yard. Into that small village Tallard put a strong garrison of infantry, with eighteen more battalions in reserve outside it and twelve squadrons of dismounted dragoons, whose horses had died of glanders, to man the gap between Blenheim and the Danube. A small stream called the Meulweyer ran through the village, while not many yards to the east of it the Nebel, just before it joined the Danube, ran swiftly enough to drive two watermills. They might also, thought Tallard, be useful as redoubts. He had time too to position his ninety cannon, some of them being hidden in the Lutzingen woods.

It was a strong position; and numerically too they had an advantage, some 56,000 Franco-Bavarians facing our poly-glot army of 52,000, of whom not more than 9,000 were British. Their 79 battalions and 140 squadrons compared with our 65 battalions and 160 squadrons; their 90 cannon outnumbering ours by 30.

Marlborough, after weighing up all this and questioning those familiar with the ground, realised that it was now or never and decided to reap the undoubted advantage of a surprise attack. 'In the case of one army attacking another', writes Kane, 'there is something unaccountable in it; for though the army attacked has the advantage of ground which they have made choice of, and very often more numerous in troops, yet it is rarely known but that the army which attacks does assuredly get the victory'; and he goes on to stress those 'unforeseen accidents which attend all battles', the outcome 'greatly depending on the ready genius and conduct of the general and the goodness of the troops he commands'. To which a more recent writer adds, 'When the opportunity came, Marlborough took the right risk at the right time, without hesitation. This was the use of genius, but it would not have been enough without the more solid qualities which gave him an army well disciplined and well supplied to lead the enemy in a race across Europe and to defeat them'.* There are times and this was one of them when Marlborough would seem to have known his men's potentialities better than they did themselves. He saw them as tough soldiers, dogged, aggressive, invincible, driving the enemy before them; while they saw him not as a demi-god but as a man in every crisis to be counted on, the man called among themselves the Old Corporal or Corporal John. Lediard calls him 'a man formed by Nature to lead a nation of heroes'.

Part of the eve-of-battle night Marlborough spent in prayer. Inevitably one thinks of Henry V before Agin-court: 'O God of battles, steel my soldiers' hearts; possess them not with fear . . .' Towards morning Marlborough received the sacrament from Francis Hare and gave orders that all the other chaplains should 'say prayers at the head of their respective regiments and implore the blessing of God upon this great undertaking'. Marlborough, says Archdeacon Coxe, felt a deep and awful sense of responsi-bility, for the crisis appeared to involve the fate of the Christian world. By a strange sort of prescience that same night the Emperor Leopold was moved to send for the Bishop of Vienna and to order him to begin next morning three days of solemn intercession for the protection of his army; for in those days, he said, the fate of the House of Austria would be decided. Marlborough is said to have slept a little before making his final arrangements with Eugene. He is also quoted as having said, as he mounted his horse, 'This day I conquer or die'. That however Sir Winston has rightly rejected; for the histrionic was never Marlborough's line.

For the rest, as one reads with what manifest gladness these men marched to battle, one wonders how dearly or how cheaply they held life: in its normal course, in those days, short and comfortless enough, if not actually painful. The instinct to live no doubt was as strong then as it always

* David Francis: *op. cit.*

70

has been, but for one reason or another courage was high. Few can have been like the Salamander (Lord Cutts), at his best in the furnace of the enemy's fire; and fewer still as devout as Blackader who, marching towards the enemy, was so successful in exercising his 'lively faith' that he found himself 'easy, sedate and cheerful'. Nothing could shake him. 'I believed firmly', he goes on, 'that his angels had me in charge and that not a bone should be broken. During all the little intervals of action I kept looking to God for strength and courage and had a plentiful through-bearing both to keep up my own heart and help to discharge my duty well in my station. My faith was so lively during the action that I sometimes said within myself, Lord, it were easy for thee to cause thy angels to lay all these men dead on the place where they stand or bring them in all prisoners to us. And for encouraging our regiment [the Cameronians, then Ferguson's] I spoke it aloud'.

If God be for us, who can be against us? One begins to feel sorry for the losing side, now due for the shock of their lives.

The Comte de Mérode-Westerloo, a Flemish cavalry general in Louis XIV's army, had enjoyed himself the evening before. After riding out beyond Blenheim and into the stubble-filled plain, he returned to camp in that village, where he sat down to a good dish of hot soup with his generals and colonels. Never, thought he, had he been in better form; and after dining and wining well, never had he slept more soundly. Nothing is said of silver wine-fountains; but when the count had, as now, to sleep in a barn, he could at least reckon on having a bed with curtains. His account continues:

Upon my orders the valet had set up my camp bed in a barn, and there I spent the night, whilst my servants lodged in the main farm building. I slept deeply until six in the morning, when I was abruptly awoken by one of my old retainers (the head groom in fact) who rushed into the barn all out of breath. He had just returned from taking my horses out to grass at four in the morning . . . This fellow, Lefranc, shook me awake and blurted out that the enemy were there. Thinking to mock him I asked, 'Where? There?' and he at once replied, 'Yes, there – there!' flinging wide as he spoke the door of the barn and drawing my bed-curtains. The door opened straight on to the fine, sunlit plain beyond, and the whole area appeared to be covered by enemy squadrons. I rubbed my eyes in disbelief and then coolly remarked that the foe must at least give me time to take my morning cup of chocolate. Whilst I was hurriedly drinking this and getting dressed, my horses were saddled and harnessed.

Clattering out of Blenheim with two aides-de-camp and thirteen spare chargers the Count noticed that everyone else was still snug in his tent, and this with the enemy close enough for his standards to be counted! They seemed to fill the whole plain, from Lutzingen woods to the Danube. Could anything stop them? Then at last the alarm was given. Tallard ordered the trumpet-calls 'To horse' and 'Boot and saddle' to be sounded repeatedly and everyone sprang to arms.

Eye-witnesses on our side take up the story. 'We lay on our arms all night', wrote Captain Parker of the Royal Irish (then Hamilton's), 'and marched by break of day in eight columns up to the enemy'. On that morning of August 13th near Tapfheim a ninth column, including the two brigades of Rowe's and Ferguson's, all under Lord Cutts, joined them and marched through a dangerous defile. Forty squadrons of cavalry rode ahead; while Colonel Blood with his artillery and pontoons took the road with Marlborough's coach and six at their tail.

The march was quite a long one – at least nine miles – the mist in our favour (as were later the sun and the wind), and

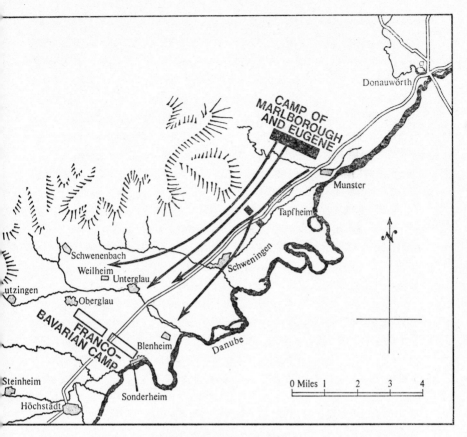

The March to Battle

then suddenly there they all were: a forest of tents still standing, 'so little did they expect a visit from us this morning'. Directly they saw us they struck camp and bundled some of their tents away to Höchstädt, half a mile to their rear. Even then however they were by no means certain that we meant to attack them, for it still seemed unthinkable. Tallard's complacency indeed, while he wrote to his king on the battle morning, was quite astonishing. At seven a.m., when our troops were within two miles of him, he added a postscript about our probable objective (Nördlingen) and sent off the messenger.

73

An hour later, when Marlborough had begun to draw up his battle-lines, Tallard, Marsin and the Elector hurriedly ascended the church tower of Blenheim to view our dispositions and, belatedly, decide what to do.

Again, peering through a small window in that narrow spire, they could not agree. The Elector wanted Tallard to post his troops 'close to the morass [on Tallard's side of the Nebel] and not suffer a man to pass but what came on the point of his bayonets. Marsin', adds Parker, 'was of the same opinion; but Tallard, a proud, conceited Frenchman, puffed up with the success of his former campaign, thought the Elector took upon him to dictate to him, and told him that was not the way to obtain a complete victory . . . He was for drawing up the army at some distance from the morass, and then the more that came over to them, the more they should kill'. There was no time to argue; and so, 'much dissatisfied', the Elector and his troops made for Lutzingen where, with Marsin on his right and both 'close to the morass', they would glare at Eugene across the Nebel, while Tallard filled the long gap between Marsin and the Danube.

Tallard's plan seems to have been as follows. When Marlborough had crossed the Nebel, Tallard and Marsin would trap him between two fires: between Tallard's at Blenheim and in the two watermills, and Marsin's at Oberglau. The attacks of those village garrisons would be followed up by a massed charge of the French cavalry on what was left of the allied centre, with a final result of rout and chaos. As a plan it could hardly be faulted; but then, as Parker goes on to say, Marlborough, 'a man of uncommon penetration and presence of mind, soon perceived Tallard's design' and took measures to thwart him. He saw too the weakness of Tallard's dispositions: the separate armies under rival commanders, not welded and integrated; the weakness in the centre, where cavalry not strongly supported with infantry might find themselves unable to summon reserves from the wings.

As Mr David Chandler has written, 'It would probably be wrong to assert that Marlborough worked out a detailed plan before the opening of the battle; but no doubt his trained eye appreciated the flaws in the French position'.*

Marlborough's left and centre were ready by ten, but Eugene was seriously delayed. Coxe describes the ground he had to cover as extremely broken, covered with brushwood and intersected by streams and rivulets, so that his troops had to make a wide circuit, and during much of it were exposed to heavy fire. But was there more to it even than that? What if, in his attempt, agreed with Marlborough, to kid the enemy into believing that the allies were bound for Nördlingen Eugene, travelling northward, had marched so far, when he decided the feint had succeeded and turned south-westward for Lutzingen, that he found himself and his army faced with a long march against time through thickets, swamps and forest: a nightmare obstacle-race, exhausting for both infantry and cavalry, towards a battle-field where the English and the rest were being bombarded? 'Rumour in the countryside expects them at Nördlingen' - so Tallard had written to Louis XIV early that morning; and today, in the Blenheim neighbourhood, this tradition of Eugene's overacted bluff lives on.

Eugene was to have been ready to attack, near Lutzingen, by eleven, but at that time and for three-quarters of an hour afterwards the allies saw no sign of him. At long last, soon after twelve, Cadogan brought Marlborough the news that Eugene was nearly in position; and then an aide-de-camp, galloping up, gave the further assurance that the Prince would give the signal at half-past twelve.

If uncertainty was, as he secretly owned, what gave Marlborough most uneasiness, then these hours of waiting for Eugene, with the troops under fire, must have been

* Chandler: *The Campaign of 1704* ('History Today', January 1963).

agony indeed; although at the time no one except perhaps Cadogan is likely to have guessed it. Sergeant Milner recalled that 'both armies cannonaded each other very smartly and vigorously with several batteries from 8 a.m. till past 12 with great loss'.* Through the eyes of his chaplain we see Marlborough on his grey charger - himself in scarlet and gold, slashed with the blue ribbon of the Garter - composedly inspecting his troops:

> His Grace now rode along the lines to observe their posture and the countenance of his men and found both them and the officers of all nations very cheerful and impatient of coming to closer engagement with the enemy. And as he was passing in the front of the first line, a large cannonball from one of the enemy's batteries grazed upon a ploughed land close by his horse's side and almost covered him with dust. He never altered his pace, but moved on and finding everything in order, sat down at length to refresh himself.

Because of the cannonade, Marlborough ordered the infantry to lie down in their ranks. Those who could had a snack. But the pioneers had to throw pontoons across the Nebel, while Blood and his artillerymen brought up their cannon to plant counter-batteries. When this last had been done, Marlborough himself rode from battery to battery and inspected it. At the same time surgeons, Hare tells us, were 'posted in convenient places'.

Where those convenient places can have been is not easy to imagine; and indeed, but for the Blenheim tapestry - the most famous of them all: that so oddly headed HOOGHSTET - the imagination, even with the help of contemporary description, would be strained indeed. In the foreground of that tapestry, between the two burning watermills, we see an improvised aid-post, with surgeons and stretcher-bearers.

* Milner, Sergeant John: *A Compendious Journal of All the Marches, Famous Battles and Sieges of the Confederate Allies in their Late War.*

For the rest, in that whole vast plain (the lines of battle stretched for nearly four miles from Blenheim on our left to Lutzingen on our extreme right), there is today no hedge and there are very few trees; the distances even from village to village, at least for infantry, look daunting. Woods are on the skyline, among rolling hills. The Danube, diverted and canalised, is now out of sight. The flat fields, then stubble, are still cultivated; there is haymaking; there is hoeing of endless rows; but except in the red and white villages there is no hint of refuge or shelter for man or beast. It is a pitiless landscape, arid and landlocked. Blenheim was fought on a very hot day; and now too, even on a sunshine day in midsummer, the prospect is intimidating.

But in the tapestry, which represents the final stage of the battle, all is or at least seems different. On the left, three villages - Blenheim, Sonderheim, Höchstädt - stand close behind each other on the near bank of the Danube, into which the Nebel flows. Two watermills on the Nebel, set on fire by the French, burn fiercely; while for the rest, amid smoke and fire the whole landscape, from Blenheim to Lutzingen, is filled with troops; the village of Blenheim itself being the most tightly packed of all. Thanks to Tallard, and still more to the Marquis de Clérambault, whom he had put in charge of that section, crack regiments like that of Navarre, waiting to rush out of the village to trap Marlborough, were 'so pent up and crowded that they had not room to make use of their arms'. Hare mentions an entrenchment, hurriedly thrown up by the French on the outskirts of Blenheim. They had also, he tells us, 'lined all the pales and hedges about that town [sic], and to make them the stronger they had taken all the tables, doors, planks, chests, etc., out of the houses and placed them so as to cover them from our shot. On that side of Blenheim which was next the Danube and the most open they had made a barricade with waggons, wheels and pieces of wood laid across to cover their retreat or at least against our Horse in case of their being forced'. In the small gap between Blenheim and the Danube Tallard posted, behind waggons, a brigade of dismounted dragoons; while in the churchyard infantry manned the walls and trampled the graves. Across the Meulweyer, the small stream which flowed through Blenheim and now runs underground to the Danube, bridges were thrown to help communications. Clérambault was told that the village must be defended if need be to the last man.

For those within it the village did at least give some protection. For the others, thousand upon thousand of them in full battle-array, opposed across the Nebel, they were without cover and 'so close to one another that they exchanged fanfares of trumpet-calls and rolls of kettle-drums, whilst the French, following their usual deplorable custom, set fire to all the villages, mills and hamlets to our front, and flames and smoke billowed up to the clouds'.

6

The Battle Begins

The fatal Day its mighty Course began
That the griev'd World had long desir'd in vain . . .
The Day was come when Heaven design'd to show
His Care and Conduct of the World below.

ADDISON, *The Campaign*

At half-past twelve Eugene sent an aide-de-camp to Marlborough to tell him he was ready; whereupon Marlborough mounted his horse and sent the young Prince of Hesse with orders to Lord Cutts to launch the attack upon the village of Blenheim. To those five British battalions, desperate for shelter from French fire, even if it was in the bed of the Nebel, the command to advance must have come as a relief. At last they could move and with a chance to retaliate. They were led on foot by their brigadier, General Rowe.

'And he had proceeded closely and slowly', says Hare, 'within thirty paces of the pales about Blenheim before the enemy gave their first fire. When this was given there fell a great many brave officers and soldiers, but yet that did not discourage that gallant officer Brigadier Rowe from marching directly to the very pales, in which he struck his sword before he suffered a man to fire a piece; and then our men gave the first volley in the teeth of the enemy. His orders were to enter sword in hand, but the superiority of the enemy and the advantage of their post made it impossible. And therefore this first line was forced to retire, but without the Brigadier who, being shot in the thigh, was left by the side of the pales. This was a great disadvantage to the service at the first beginning; and his own Lieutenant-Colonel and

79

Major, who best knew his worth, endeavouring to fetch him off, were both killed upon the spot'.

Hare makes no mention of the two watermills on the Nebel, taken by our troops as they crossed it towards Blenheim. These were being used as redoubts by the enemy, who set them on fire just before they abandoned them.

At this early stage it may have looked as though Tallard's scheme was going to work. Blenheim held, and now some of his infantry burst out of it, while his crack cavalry, the *Gendarmerie*, sweeping round the north-east corner of the village, routed Rowe's regiment and captured its colours. At that moment however a brigade of Hessians, forming our second line, came to the rescue, snatched back the colours and drove the enemy back to their lines.

Further charges and counter-charges followed and with such violence that the Marquis de Clérambault, the officer in command of Blenheim village, ordered, first, seven battalions and later another eleven of Tallard's infantry reserves, posted by him outside the village, to enter and stay within its pales and hedges. It has been said that de Clérambault gave this fatal order without referring to Tallard. It could be however that his messenger never reached him. According to one authority, Tallard, 'much against his will and in a very wrong time', was visiting Marsin and the Elector, on his extreme left, 'that he might be the better judge of the dispositions made there'.

Once all those battalions - some twenty-seven of them - had been boxed into Blenheim, obviously the best possible plan for the allies was to keep them there, out of the rest of the battle. For the time being therefore it was Cutts's responsibility and Churchill's to see that the English, the Hessians and the Dutch posted north and east of the village (in all some twenty battalions and fifteen squadrons) kept all exits from Blenheim closed; and this, partly by keeping up feigned attacks, they did. 'During the remainder of the day', adds Trevelyan, 'Blenheim contained, dead and alive, about twelve thousand of the best infantry of France'.

Even when at a time of crisis Mérode-Westerloo tried to persuade de Clérambault to let him withdraw twelve battalions from Blenheim to defend the Nebel, he was refused. Thanks to accurate, platoon-firing,* the Count goes on to say, not a single shot of ours missed its mark; while those French troops at the barricades who were able to return the fire soon became too exhausted to reload, even if their muskets, from repeated use, had not exploded. What made things still worse was that some of the thatch in the village was blazing, so that amid collapsing beams and roofs not a few French soldiers were burned alive.

'All this while', Hare remembers, 'both armies continued to cannon one another very briskly'. Forty miles off the din was heard at Ingoldstadt by the Margrave of Baden who, writing to the Emperor, added: 'The Prince and the Duke are engaged today to the westward. Heaven bless them'.

*

To Tallard Blenheim village, the stronghold on his flank, might seem all-important. But the vitals of his army, as Marlborough realised, lay in the centre and it was on that part of the long and too thinly covered front where, thanks to the battalions cooped up in Blenheim, Tallard's cavalry lacked strong infantry-support, that Marlborough concentrated. Already, during the first attack on Blenheim, Churchill's infantry had been ordered to begin crossing the Nebel there, near the village of Unterglau, on our side of the stream, which was in flames. That crossing, with fascines and pontoons (they made five bridges) was not easy; its most hazardous part the re-forming on the enemy side and then

---

* The line infantry fired by platoons, instead of by rank or even battalion volleys, as was the continued practice of the French and their allies. This innovation gave the English the advantage of a higher and more accurate rate of fire, based upon a far more effective direction of fire control by the sergeants and subordinate officers. An additional advantage lay in the fact that at any one time a third of the battalion was ready loaded . . . The delayed volley, followed by the bayonet charge into the reeling enemy ranks, became the battle-winning formula. Chandler: *The Marlborough Wars*, App. I.

turning to cover three squadrons of British cavalry under Colonel Palmes which, breaking into columns, rode down to the stream before dismounting to lead their horses by the bridle across the bridges and fords. Marlborough himself followed with further squadrons.

Sergeant Milner remembers: 'Our left wing cavalry passed the rivulet pell-mell in the centre, as did our right, having made several passages with diverse pieces of wood which they had found at hand ... So all passed and drew up in order of battle as well as the ground would permit on the other side of the rivulet. The enemy gave us all the time we wanted for that purpose and kept very quiet on the hill they were possessed of, without descending to the meadow towards the rivulet, insomuch that even our second line of Horse had time to form themselves; and to this capital fault of the French we ought principally to ascribe the victory'.

This of course was the enemy's chance for a major slaughter. He failed to take it. Kane sees Tallard, at this moment, as a man infatuated, who looked on but, as one dazed, seemed unable to give the command to fire. 'If they have not bridges enough', he is reported to have said, 'I will lend them some ... Let them pass'; and then, repeating his words to Marsin and the Elector before the battle, 'The more that come over, the more we shall have to kill'.

Marlborough, on the other hand, was preparing to teach the armies of Europe a lesson in new tactics, in cavalry-and-infantry 'interlining', a system which had been made workable by the adoption of the flintlock and the ring-bayonet. Of the four lines drawn up under Churchill, here at the centre of Marlborough's army, the front (thirteen battalions) and the back (ten battalions) were of infantry, the second and third (seventy-one squadrons) cavalry, to cover each other. This mutual protection made for good morale. When the cavalry charged, gaps were left in the infantry lines for them to return into and, should they still be pursued, the infantry could discourage their pursuers not

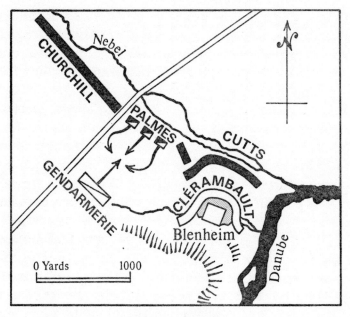

Palmes's Charge

only with platoon-volleys but, when the front rank dropped to one knee and dug the butts of their bayoneted muskets into the ground, with a terrifying obstacle, for enemy horses, in the shape of a hedge of steel.

But long before all our troops had crossed the Nebel and re-formed, Tallard had pulled himself together and given the signal for eight squadrons of the *Gendarmerie* to ride down Palmes's five squadrons and cut them to pieces; for as Captain Parker testifies, Tallard 'verily thought there were not any on earth able to stand before them'. He was to be disappointed. Zurlauben, the Swiss Lieutenant-General in command of the *Gendarmerie*, ordered them to edge outward before suddenly wheeling in upon Palmes's flanks; but Palmes foresaw this and directed his left and right to wheel outward and charge the squadrons descending upon them from that slightly higher ground. After routing them, he said, they might then wheel in upon the flanks of the rest. The very notion of such a manoeuvre, outnumbered and outpositioned as they were, was audacity itself. With none but first-class cavalry, perfectly drilled, could the thing have been contemplated; and it succeeded so well that not only were the *Gendarmerie* routed, with Zurlauben mortally wounded, but as a result of seeing his own crack troops in flight, Tallard's morale, as he afterwards admitted, was profoundly undermined. The Elector of Bavaria too was mortified. 'What!' he exclaimed, 'the *Gendarmerie* running away, is it possible? Go, gentlemen, tell them that I am here in person. Rally them and lead them back to the charge'.

Trevelyan pays tribute too to the infantry, and not only Churchill's but the Germans', largely responsible as they were, in spite of setbacks and temporary retreats, for steady progress in the centre and for enabling the cavalry there to reform after their repulse. But indeed, as Marlborough himself wrote after the battle to Robert Harley, 'The bravery of all our troops on this occasion cannot be expressed; the generals as well as the officers and soldiers behaving themselves with the greatest courage and resolution, the horse and dragoons having been obliged to charge four or five several times'.

In the centre where, under Marlborough, Churchill commanded, charge and counter-charge followed; for as even Tallard by now had realised, to let the enemy cross the Nebel unhindered and then, as Mérode-Westerloo put it, 'calmly charge and attack us as if we were babes in arms', was crass folly. General Lumley, bringing across squadrons of cavalry, played an unenviable role; for the Nebel just there was a two-branched stream with a marsh in the middle, and when stream and bog had been crossed, the reception was so hot – a Blenheim battery raking their flank while cavalry charged their front – that they were forced to retire as best they could. The fighting now became as fierce as it had been at the Schellenberg. Firing – musket, cannonball, case-shot

– broke out everywhere, from one end of the front to the
other:

> Now from each Van
> The brazen Instruments of Death discharge
> Horrible Flames, and turbid streaming Clouds
> Of Smoke sulphureous; intermix't with these
> Large globous Irons fly, of dreadful Hiss,
> Singeing the Air, and from long Distance bring
> Surprising Slaughter; on each Side they fly
> By Chains connex't, and with destructive Sweep
> Behead whole Troops at once; the hairy Scalps
> Are whirl'd aloof, while numerous Trunks bestrow
> Th'ensanguin'd Field; with latent Mischief stor'd
> Show'rs of Granadoes rain, by sudden Burst
> Disploding murd'rous Bowels, fragments of Steel
> And Stones and Glass and nitrous Grain adust.
> A Thousand Ways at once the shiver'd Orbs
> Fly diverse, working Torment and foul Rout
> With deadly Bruise and Gashes furrow'd deep.
> Of Pain impatient the high prancing Steeds
> Disdain the Curb and flinging to and fro
> Spurn their dismounted Riders; they expire
> Indignant, by unhostile Wounds destroy'd.
> Thus thro' each Army Death in various Shapes
> Prevail'd; here mangl'd Limbs, here Brains and Gore
> Lie clotted; lifeless Some; with Anguish these
> Gnashing, and loud Laments invoking Aid,
> Unpity'd and unheard; the louder Din
> Of Guns and Trumpets clang and solemn Sound
> Of Drums o'ercame their Groans. In equal Scale
> Long hung the Fight, few Marks of Fear were seen,
> None of Retreat . . .*

*

* John Philips: *Blenheim.*

The whole front was in uproar, the fight at its fiercest now about Oberglau, a village on Marlborough's right, defended by Marsin and his able lieutenant, de Blainville. When ten battalions of Churchill's infantry, under the Prince of Holstein-Beck, attempted to cross the Nebel and storm the village, de Blainville, with nine battalions including the Irish mercenaries known as the Wild Geese, attacked them. The Prince, threatened too on his right by Marsin's cavalry, asked to be reinforced from Eugene's left wing of cuirassiers, but they themselves were hard pressed. Holstein-Beck, mortally wounded, was taken prisoner and two of his battalions were overwhelmed.

By this one stroke, simple though it was, our whole line was threatened with division and rupture. It was a situation where dismay could easily have led to despair and panic; but the possibility of such a crisis had not been overlooked. In the Blenheim tapestry we see Marlborough at a point of vantage, with his aides-de-camp and, at his horse's head, one of his team of running footmen, blue-tunicked and peak-capped like an unmounted jockey: swift-footed youths, hand-picked and, as a news team, virtually invented by Marlborough himself. From experience he knew the value of minute-to-minute knowledge on the battlefield; and so, as Mr Chandler first discovered, his system of communication was original and two-fold. First to be relied on were his mounted A.D.C.'s, trained as they were to ride from post to post, to sum up each situation and to bring him word of exactly what was happening behind, as often as not, clouds of black smoke. In bright coats and on horseback they made obvious targets and quite often they were killed. Then came the turn of the young runners with their long staffs - gold-topped, silver-topped, bronze-topped, according to seniority - who, again to quote Chandler, 'belted about the battle-field', dodging horses and cannonballs, and then looking and listening before racing back with the news.

Within minutes of their having pantingly poured their

findings into Marlborough's ear he would as if by magic appear just where he was desperately needed, there to direct the storm. And so it was at Oberglau. Leaving the smoke of Unterglau and crossing the Nebel, Marlborough quickly led to the rescue three Hanoverian battalions and at the same time directed Colonel Blood to bring up a battery of cannon: twelve three-tonners, to be manhandled over the Nebel marshes. The Wild Geese were resisted and driven back.

But Marsin, a better general than Tallard, was not to be so easily repulsed. Observing that some of Holstein-Beck's troops were still crossing or re-forming, he rallied his cavalry and ordered another charge upon the right flank of Marlborough's centre. Marlborough's A.D.C. promptly galloped to Eugene for reinforcements. They could not be spared - Eugene, beyond Oberglau, was already out-numbered by two to one - but they were instantly sent. General Fugger's Imperial cuirassiers, changing front, charged to meet Marsin's cavalry and hurled them back in disorder. Even then the threat to Oberglau and the centre was not over. Tallard had seen, as he wrote afterwards, the hope of victory ('I saw one instant in which the battle was won if the cavalry had not turned and abandoned the infantry of the line'); while on our side, as Hare later told his cousin, 'The French . . . pressed our men so hard that before three I thought we had lost the day'. But that would have been reckoning without Lord Orkney, 'who went to the head of several squadrons and got 'em to rally'; and without Blood's cannon, which now answered the enemy's with case and grape. Under their cover Marlborough used his Hanoverians like sheepdogs, rounding up de Blainville's troops and, to borrow Sir Winston's analogy, penning them in Oberglau as Tallard's were being penned by Cutts in Blenheim. The crisis was over.

Coxe calls it a prompt and masterly movement. By it, he says, Marlborough linked his army with Eugene's and at the same time, while those three Hanoverian battalions divided the attention of the enemy and protected Eugene's left, forming above Oberglau, they covered the right of the main body of cavalry and masked the offensive movement which Marlborough was planning against Tallard.

It was now three in the afternoon. After six hours of almost continuous fire there was a lull.

*

If resistance was stubborn on our left at Blenheim and in the central part of the front at Oberglau, it was toughest of all on our right, where Eugene was in command. After forcing their way through thicket and forest to their battle positions, his eighteen battalions and ninety-two squadrons found themselves faced, across rivulets and marshes, by twenty-nine battalions and sixty-seven squadrons led by the enemy's ablest commander the Elector of Bavaria. The distance between the opposing forces was about 600 yards.

Marlborough's plan as we now see it: to attack first on the flanks and finally in the centre (the reverse of the Schellenberg scheme) was sound enough. He successfully repeated it at Ramillies and at Malplaquet. But what if his irresistible forces met immovable objects? On his left Blenheim village, solid with Tallard's troops, looked impregnable. In the centre Marsin's men still blazed away from the shelter of Oberglau. True, most of them were immobilised, but so were the regiments left to guard them. And now on the right Eugene for all his efforts could make little progress. As at Blenheim and at Oberglau, his was in fact, as Trevelyan puts it, a containing action, gallantly performed and essential to Marlborough's victory elsewhere.

The Prince of Anhalt, commanding Eugene's infantry, which included Danes and Prussians, was, as has been seen, outnumbered by two to one. After crossing the Nebel with the object of taking the enemy in flank, his men, waiting for their artillery, came well within range of a

Bavarian battery in front of Lutzingen. They could not move until a counter-battery had been planted at the edge of the firwoods. Then they advanced in columns, crossed the marsh and re-formed in battle-order on the enemy side. At great cost the Prussians then carried the battery, while Eugene's cavalry forded the stream and drove the first line of the Bavarian cavalry through the second. But the second line of their cavalry rallied and drove Eugene's back across the Nebel and to the edge of the woods. Worse was to follow. The Bavarians, wheeling left, took the Prussian infantry in flank and recovered the cannon. Even then what was left of the Prussian regiment resisted, only to be driven back with heavy loss. The Danes, who had gained some ground near the woods, were forced to leave it. Only the intervention of Anhalt, who rushed in and rallied his men, prevented a general rout.

Eugene had no better success with his cavalry. Again and again he led them across stream and marsh to charge the enemy but, unsupported as they were by their hard-pressed infantry and under fire from Oberglau as well as from Lutzingen, they were repeatedly driven back across the Nebel. How marshy was the Nebel? Writing afterwards on the same day (August 25, 1704) Prince Eugene refers to it as 'un ruisseau fort difficile à passer'; whereas the Baron de Montigny-Languet maintains that it was only two feet broad and made a little marsh, much dried up by the drought. Most of the French generals, he adds, had supposed it worse. Other accounts make it clear that the Nebel was easy enough for infantry to cross in some places (e.g. the Blenheim watermills), but in others steep banks and bogs called for fascines and pontoons to get the cavalry across.

On both sides exhaustion had set in; and there they were, their horses' sides heaving, themselves pausing and panting and, as Coxe says, 'at such a small distance as enabled every individual to mark the countenance of his opponent. In this awful suspense the Elector was seen emulating the conduct of Eugene, riding from rank to rank, encouraging the brave and rousing the timid by his voice and example'.

At last Eugene's cavalry were to be supported by infantry. Anhalt, changing front, advanced obliquely, his right towards the woods, to take the Bavarians in flank. Eugene signalled the Horse to charge again; but after their double repulse they had lost heart. For the third time their line was broken and in utter confusion they fled beyond the Nebel.

At this point Eugene's bearing may be compared with Marlborough's, the latter 'giving his orders', as Kane saw him in times of crisis, 'with all the calmness imaginable'. Eugene, says Coxe, was now in a transport of despair as he left the Prince of Hanover and the Duke of Wirtemberg to rally the Horse while he galloped to the infantry, who were still attacking with incredible resolution. Frustrated beyond endurance, indifferent to death, Eugene rode into the open and came within seconds of being shot by a Bavarian dragoon. An Imperialist however, seeing the dragoon take aim, cut him down with his sabre. There is a story, probably apocryphal, that in his Italian rage Eugene chased two horsemen of his own regiment, as they fled from the enemy, and shot them dead. But whatever the truth of the matter, his infantry rallied again, turned the left flank of the enemy and with much bloodshed drove them back through the woods beyond Lutzingen. It was now past four and neither side could do more than glare at each other. 'I have not a squadron or a battalion', Eugene said afterwards, 'which did not charge four times at least'.

*

But let Hare take up the tale of what was happening in the centre:

The Duke of Marlborough had got the whole of the left wing of the allied army over the rivulet, and our Horse

Allied troops cross the Nebel

Prince Eugene of Savoy

John Churchill, Duke of Marlborough

Marshal Tallard

Field dressing station by the burning watermill on the Nebel

were drawn up in two lines fronting that of the enemy; but they did not offer to charge till General Churchill had ranged all the Foot also in two lines behind the cavalry. That general, as soon as he had got over the rivulet, had inclined to the left, extending himself towards Blenheim and leaving intervals for our squadrons to pass through in case of a repulse. Perceiving however that the enemy had intermingled some regiments of Foot with their cavalry immediately on the right of Oberglau . . . he ordered some Hanoverian regiments of Foot to halt and make head against the enemy's infantry; and Colonel Blood was ordered at the same time to march a battery of cannon over the pontoons and bring it to bear upon the enemy's battalions. This was done with good success and made a great slaughter of the enemy. They stood firm however for a time, closing their ranks as fast as they were broken, till being much weakened they were at last thrown into disorder, when our squadrons falling upon them, they were cut down in entire ranks and were seen so lying after the battle.

In that part of the front the French infantry had, as Trevelyan says, been reduced to a handful of boys who knew nothing of battles except how to die at their post. 'Supported by nobody', he adds, 'they died to a man where they stood'.

'From a church tower', wrote Mérode-Westerloo, 'you would have seen the enemy repulsed on one flank and us on the other, the battle rippling to and fro like the waves of the sea, with the entire line engaged in hand-to-hand combat from one end to the other - a rare enough occurrence. All this took place under a deadly hail of fire from the infantry, especially during the various attacks on the villages and hamlets, as well as on Blenheim and the other sectors under attack in the centre. This spectacle, lit by bright sunlight, must have been magnificent for any spectator in a position to view it with sangfroid'.

At the time he writes of, nearing five in the afternoon, the Count was about to need all the sangfroid he could muster, for even as he was rallying the remnants of his cavalry for another charge, he saw the enemy, at his leisure, calmly drawing up a complete battle-array in the very centre of his army. This in fact was the climax Marlborough had almost certainly from the outset planned for. Left and right had been dealt with: Cutts could be counted on to contain Blenheim, while on the right near Lutzingen the Elector was fully occupied with Eugene. At five or soon after the moment came for the main attack in the centre.

7

Havoc

Thousands of fiery Steeds with Wounds transfix'd,
Floating in Gore, with their dead Masters mixt,
Midst Heaps of Spears and Standards driv'n around,
Lie in the Danube's bloody Whirlpools drown'd.
ADDISON, *The Campaign*

Marlborough rode along the front and gave orders to sound the charge; whereupon the two lines of allied cavalry, sword in hand, moved forward.

Sergeant Milner describes the attack as he saw it:

The Horse of our left going towards the hill, that of the enemy began to move at last and charge our men with a great deal of fury. The French Foot at Blenheim at the same time from behind the hedges made a terrible fire on the flank of our Horse, who were advanced too near to that village . . . and were put into such disorder that some of them retired beyond the rivulet. General Bülow then brought up his Lunenburg dragoons and some troops of Zell and charged with such vigour that they drove the enemy beyond the second rivulet called Meulweyer and from thence to the very hedges of Blenheim. This gave time to our men that had given ground to repass the rivulet and form a second line behind those dragoons who remained in the first line all the remaining time of the action.

The Horse of our left, having by this success gained the advantage of forming themselves entirely in order of battle, advanced leisurely to the top of the hill and charged several times the enemy's Horse, who were always

93

routed, yet nevertheless rallied every time though at a considerable distance, which gave us opportunity to gain ground; and as we were preparing for a fresh attack, Tallard caused ten battalions to advance and fill up the intervals of his Horse in order to make a last effort, which the Prince of Hesse Cassel, Generals Lumley, Bülow, Hompesch and Ingoldsby perceiving, caused three battalions of the troops of Zell to come up and sustain our Horse, and then we returned to the charge; but by the superiority of the enemy's Foot our first line was put somewhat in disorder, so that it shrank back about sixty paces . . . neither advancing against the other, but at last our men renewed the charge and routed the enemy's Horse, and the ten battalions abandoned by them were entirely cut to pieces, none escaping but a few who threw themselves on the ground as dead, to save their lives.

Their opponents were by now, as Parker testifies, in a tottering condition; and our cavalry had been well briefed. They were to advance gently until they came pretty near to them. 'And this they did', Parker adds, 'so effectually that it decided the fate of the day. The French fire was quite extinguished, they made not the least resistance but gave way and broke at once. Our squadrons drove through the very centre of them, which put them to an entire rout. About thirty of their squadrons made toward a bridge of boats they had over the Danube; but the bridge (as it frequently happens in such cases) broke under the crowd that rushed upon it, and down they went. At the same time our squadrons pursued close at their heels, cutting down all before them; for in all such close pursuits 'tis very rare that any quarter is given. In short, they were almost all of them killed or drowned'.

Marlborough himself wrote afterwards of 'upwards of thirty squadrons of the French which we pushed into the

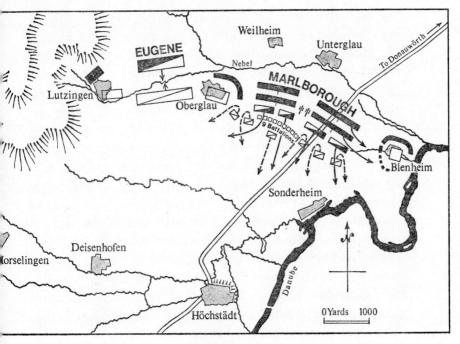

Breakthrough

Danube, where we saw the greatest part of them perish'. Between two and three thousand French cavalrymen were in fact thus accounted for. Among the luckier ones was Mérode-Westerloo, whose escape reads like melodrama:

So tight was the press that my horse was carried along some three hundred paces without putting hoof to ground, right to the edge of a deep ravine. Down we plunged a good twenty feet into a swampy meadow. My horse stumbled and fell. A moment later several men and horses fell on top of me, as the remains of my cavalry swept by, all intermingled with the hotly pursuing foe. I spent several minutes trapped beneath my horse . . . which was not dead but utterly exhausted . . . I extricated myself from the pile of dead horses that had fallen on top

95

of us both. I had barely found my feet when a passing hussar fired his pistol at me. The next moment a huge English horse-grenadier, a whole head and shoulders taller than I, came up. He dismounted and came forward to take me prisoner in a leisurely way. I noticed his lackadaisical air and grasped my long sword, which was dangling from my wrist, keeping it well pressed into my side. When he was within two paces I lunged at him, but then I discovered that my left knee was injured, so I stumbled and missed my stroke. The Englishman raised his sword to cut me down, but I parried his blow and ran my sword right through his body up to the hilt . . .'

Some of his tales must be taken with more than a pinch of salt. Obviously however he was lucky to escape, bluffing his way as he did through our ranks to his own at Höchstädt, some two miles to the rear. Other French squadrons had fled to Sonderheim, between Höchstädt and Blenheim.

A French general takes up the story:

The news of this being brought to Grignan's Brigade, which was retired more to the left to pass the morass at Höchstädt, they rallied and marched to the enemy and made them abandon the defile in which they were, and thereby disengaged all those who were not either killed or taken. They then formed themselves on the height of Höchstädt and marching on faced the enemy, which gave time to draw off the wounded from that place. This was the sad fate of a brisk and good cavalry which might have been used to better purpose; but which we give over lamenting as soon as we begin to consider the wretched destiny of our regiments of Foot.

*

For Tallard the long hot day was nearly over. The French general continues his report to his Minister for War:

Monsieur de Tallard interlaced our battalions with our

96

cavalry with design to make a last effort to break the double lines of the enemy. Our men marched up to them gallantly and the enemy's first line threw themselves on their second. We gained some ground and advanced to charge the second line, but this being sustained by a third and fourth, our troopers fled and our poor battalions were cut in pieces. We rallied again the third time the cavalry which was broken, but it was so diminished by the several charges that it now formed but one line.

Things being in this condition, Monsieur de Tallard considered that it was high time to draw off the dragoons and infantry out of the village of Blenheim and exhorting his cavalry to stand their ground, he took that resolution. He sent a trusty person to Monsieur de Marsin to desire him to face the enemy with some troops on the right of his village, to keep them in play to favour the retreat of our infantry; but he represented to the messenger that he had too much on his hands in the front of his village and the rest of the lines to think of sparing any troops, he being so far from victorious that he could but just maintain his ground.

During this discourse our Horse had faced the enemy, but on a sudden they were ordered to wheel about, which you will imagine was done with great disorder. In short, this was so precipitate a flight that many cast themselves into the Danube and the enemy let loose three regiments of dragoons after them. Monsieur de Tallard was environed with the fugitives.

Lediard noticed that the French would not admit to a great loss from drowning in the Danube - 'Monsieur de Quincy reduces the number to less than fifty' but he will have none of this. 'A whole body of their cavalry', he insists, 'the best and most renowned of their whole army, seized with the same panic, hurried away the Marshal de Tallard with them in their flight and void of all thought, threw themselves by whole squadrons into the Danube, men and horses, officers and troopers. Some few had the good fortune of escape, but much the greater part, to avoid an uncertain death which at worst could but have overtaken them in the field of battle and laid them down in the bed of honour, rushed upon a certain and ignominious death in the river.'

In a last desperate effort to reach Blenheim village and somehow free some of his infantry Tallard and his officers were swept along by French cavalry retreating from the centre. But near Sonderheim, beside the Danube, he was overtaken by Hessian dragoons, whose commanding officer (an aide-de-camp of the Prince of Hesse) spotting the Marshal's Order of the St Esprit, forced him to surrender and then conducted him to Marlborough.

This, the conquered faced with his conqueror, was the scene afterwards chosen by Marlborough for the chief of the Blenheim tapestries, himself sedate and expressionless on his fine grey, while Tallard rides up as in a nightmare, his face lined with anguish. This then was the climax, the see-saw moment of Tallard's ruin and Marlborough's triumph; a tableau to be painted and woven and sculpted, and engraved on men's minds until the end of time.

With solemn courtesy Marlborough ushered Tallard to his coach.* But what was there to say? 'I am very sorry that such a cruel misfortune should have fallen upon a soldier for whom I have had the highest regard'. And Tallard? 'I congratulate you on defeating the best soldiers in the world'. To which Marlborough of course replied, 'Your Lordship, I presume, excepts those who had the honour to beat them.'

'The taking of Monsieur de Tallard is a great misfortune for the King, for it is certain that with his infantry he might have made a very honourable retreat; whereas that

---

* Tallard wears a blue coat and a feathered hat. In Laguerre's mural of the same scene, painted on the Saloon wall at Marlborough House, Tallard wears a red coat and a tricorne with a white cockade.

infantry is now the laughing stock of nations and useless to the king for a long time in a war so violent as this', concludes the French general despondently.

*

Though victory was now certain, the battle was not yet finished. It was the moment chosen, however, by Blackader to dash off a letter home: 'I am just now retired from the noise of drums, of oaths and dying groans', he wrote to his patron, Lady Campbell of Stirling, 'I am to return in a few minutes to the field of battle and, wrapping myself up in the arms of Omnipotence, I believe myself no less safe, as to every valuable purpose, than if sitting in your Ladyship's chamber'.

On the left, Blenheim held out. On the right, the Elector and Marsin were, in Marlborough's words, 'so advantageously posted that Prince Eugene could make no impression on them till the third attack at or near seven at night'. But for a misunderstanding there would have been a bloodbath. In the failing light and in the clouds of black smoke from Lutzingen and Oberglau, their mud-spattered coats made friend and foe look alike so that, while Eugene mistook squadrons of allied cavalry under Hompesch for Tallard's, Marlborough took Eugene's troops in pursuit of the Elector for Bavarian and ordered Hompesch to halt.

Sergeant Milner gives this account of it:

The Duke of Marlborough repaired to the centre and caused part of the victorious Horse to halt. Observing the Elector retreating from Lutzingen, he ordered General Hompesch to return from his pursuit, but before he could do so, the right wing of our army was seen at some distance behind the Elector and appearing to be a part of his army marching in such a manner as might easily have flanked us had the Duke of Marlborough immediately charged him, he with great prudence sent out a party to view them . . .

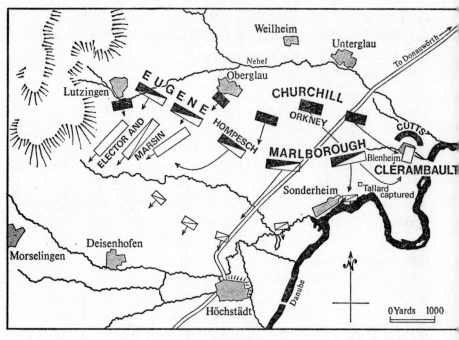

Pursuit

Turning to Prince Eugene, Milner recalls how, after the repeated repulse of his cavalry, he put himself at the head of his infantry, 'who pursued the enemy over hills, dales, rocks and woods, and having charged them again, did entirely rout them and continue to chase them for above an hour's march' . . . As for the final pursuit, Eugene and Marlborough, he says, 'would have followed with equal speed, but the great number of their prisoners was a luggage that retarded their progress four or five days'.

'Our Troops', wrote Captain Parker, 'were much fatigued, and night drew on, all which favoured the enemy's retreat. Or perhaps it may rather be said that Providence interposed, which seeing the slaughter of the day, thought it sufficient: otherwise, few if any of them could have escaped.'

In the pause that followed, Marlborough, still on horse-

back wrote with a lead pencil his brief and famous dispatch*
to Sarah his duchess:

August 13, 1704

I have not time to say more but to beg you will give my
duty to the Queen and let her know her Army has had a
Glorious Victory. M. Tallard and two other Generals are
in my coach and I am following the rest. The bearer, my
aide-de-camp Colonel Parke, will give her an account of
what has passed. I shall do it in a day or two by another
more at large.

Marlborough.

* On a nineteenth-century silver centrepiece at Blenheim Palace a running-footman
holds up a drum for Marlborough to write his dispatch. The only scrap he could find to
write on happened to be a bill in French for tavern expenses, beginning: '16 May. For
six loaves and one candle . . .'

8

Surrender

Whole Captive Hosts the Conqueror detains
In painful Bondage and inglorious Chains
ADDISON, *The Campaign*

In the evening light at Blenheim the last field - the village
itself, still packed with soldiers - now awaited harvest. Dr
Coxe found that Tallard's order to evacuate never reached
it. 'Without chief and without orders they waited their
destiny with a firmness deserving of a better fate'. Cutts had
been zealous, and so had Churchill. From the village, where
desperation grew, scarcely one had escaped, although to add
to the rest of its troubles the French garrison had since four
o'clock been leaderless. The French themselves never discovered just how or why de Clérambault, the officer in
command of all those Blenheim battalions, was drowned in
the Danube. His servant is said to have sounded the river
before his master threw himself into it, 'la tête lui ayant
tourné'. Certainly at the time none but that servant knew
of his death and so for some hours his command remained
unfilled.

Later, when in the centre the French and Bavarian cavalry
had been put to flight, Churchill sent to Lord Cutts. He
intended, he told him, attacking Blenheim in flank. Would
his Lordship, if his troops were not too worn out, be good
enough to stage a simultaneous attack on the front of the
village? Churchill then led his infantry towards Blenheim,
extending his flank to the Danube, while General Meredith
with the Queen's Regiment (later the Hampshire Regiment) took possession of a barrier on the Blenheim bank of
the river. These movements 'roused the enemy from a state

of sullen desperation'. They tried to bolt, first at the rear of the village, then towards Sonderheim, then towards Oberglau; but every outlet was blocked and every sortie repulsed either by the Scots Greys under Lord John Hay or by the cavalry and dragoons under Lumley and Ross.

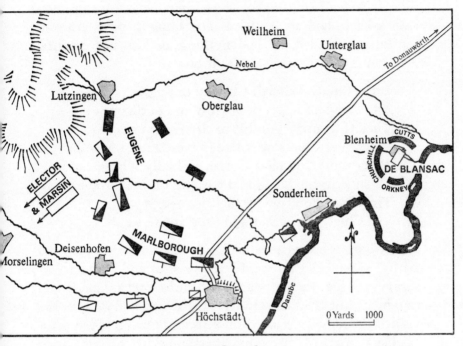

End of Battle

While Cutts guarded the exits on the side of the Nebel, the Earl of Orkney with eight battalions attacked the high-walled churchyard; and General Ingoldsby with four battalions and some of Ross's dragoons tried to storm the opening towards Oberglau. Resistance was savage.

Of some of this Tallard was a reluctant witness. On his way under escort to Marlborough's coach he begged that 'these poor fellows' might be allowed to retire. If this were granted, he added, he would himself give the command for a general cease-fire. But when Marlborough received his message he was shocked. 'Inform Monsieur de Tallard', he said, 'that in the position in which he now is he has no command'. The exchange was typical of both commanders: of Tallard, once the well-liked ambassador at St James's; and of Marlborough, the highly professional soldier. As Tallard must have realised, the shot was a long one, but for humanity's sake it had to be tried. For himself, with his son mortally wounded, he had nothing to lose but his life. Addison in *The Campaign* piles it on:

> Unfortunate Tallard! Oh who can name
> The Pangs of Rage, of Sorrow and of Shame
> That with mixt Tumult in thy Bosom swell'd
> When first thou saw'st thy Bravest Troops repell'd,
> Thine Only Son pierc'd with a Deadly Wound,
> Choak'd in his Blood and gasping on the Ground,
> Thyself in Bondage by the Victor kept!
> The Chief, the Father and the Captive wept.

Marlborough's reserves had, as he had intended, played a critical part; Tallard's were *hors de combat* and in danger of massacre. This was not war as Versailles understood it and taught it; but then how much of that day had been in the French drill-book? What of dissension between allied commanders, what of mists and marshes, what of one's own crack cavalry running away?

As for Marlborough's own officers, one wonders to what extent he, the arch-bluffer, schooled them in the sly and profitable art of bluff. Some perhaps needed no such schooling. And so it is that at this late and tricky stage of the battle one feels for those leaderless brigadiers in Blenheim village who now fell for the guile of George Hamilton, first Earl of Orkney, and his aide-de-camp Sir James Abercromby, who took it upon them to trick Louis's armed and unconquered battalions into surrender.

Orkney's men, who had twice been repulsed from the

churchyard and had set fire to another part of the village, were about to be attacked by two French brigades when on an inspired impulse, Orkney had his drums beat a parley. His own explanation sounds wonderfully bland. 'The firing of the cottages', he said, 'we could perceive annoyed them very much, and seeing two brigades appear as if they intended to cut their way out through our troops, who were very fatigued, it came into my head to beat a parley, which they accepted of immediately, and their Brigadier Dénonville capitulated with me to be prisoners at my discretion and lay down their arms'.

The French general reported to Versailles, 'The enemy, having surrounded the village of Blenheim with several lines, advanced to straighten it close on the left flank where our right of Horse was before posted. Our men were soon alarmed and the Colonel of the Royal Regiment bethought himself of saving his life and that of his soldiers, whom he caused to lay down their arms and himself surrendered the colours. The soldiers of Surlaube, who were likewise on the left flank, put themselves into disorder and entered the centre of the village in confusion. Monsieur de Sivière being informed of this disorder called the regiments of Provence and Artois and all that were resolute to him and with sword in hand drove the enemy to the very head of their cavalry and returned to the village leisurely. Monsieur de Sivière had his wrist broken'.

Dénonville, described as a young man of fashion, little acquainted with war, only stuck out for the prisoners not being plundered. This was more than good enough for Sir James Abercromby who, riding up to the Régiment Royale, snatched its colours from the ensign, who wounded him, though not badly, in the arm. 'I asked them', he said afterwards, 'if they did not hear what the General offered; but his Lordship was come up by this time, without giving any fire, and ordered them to lay down their arms, which they did asking quarter'.

But even then there was still some resistance. The Marquis de Blansac, acting as Clérambault's successor in command of the nine thousand or so French still in the village, protested against surrender while Dénonville held forth in its favour. Eventually de Blansac let Abercromby take him to Orkney just outside Blenheim, and there the game continued. Orkney, probably in good French, tried what he afterwards called a little gasconade: de Blansac was assured that, even as he was speaking, Marlborough and his army were on their way. It worked. The general order to surrender at discretion was given, at nine in the evening, and the cream of France's army had somehow to stomach it. The proud regiment of Navarre, a thousand strong, shed tears of rage as they ceremonially burned their standards to save them from capture, while others sullenly and ashamedly handed theirs over. According to the French general's report, 'The Duke of Marlborough judging rightly that there were old troops in that place, the overcoming of which would cost him dear, made use of Monsieur Dénonville his prisoner to exhort them to accept their lives. Monsieur de Blansac consented to it and did his best to get the consent of Navarre, who burned his colours. All yielded. Monsieur de Blansac signed the articles, but Sivière and Jourry refused to set their hands to them. They were all disarmed and had their colours taken from them. Grief will not suffer me to carry this recital any farther. You may well imagine what a sad spectacle it is to see six and twenty battalions and four regiments of dragoons prisoners.'

Cutts, when Abercromby brought him the news, on the east side of the village, could hardly believe it, it seemed too good to be true; for his own brigades - Rowe's, Ferguson's and the rest - were worn to a ravelling, they could have done no more. As for Orkney and Abercromby they were, as Trevelyan says, tough aristocrats and canny Scots. Orkney, married to Betty Villiers, 'perhaps the cleverest woman in England after Duchess Sarah', wrote later: 'Without

English and Allied cavalry drive the French into the Danube.
Colonel Blood's cannon in the foreground

Marshal Tallard surrenders to Marlborough

Marshal Tallard in Marlborough's coach after his capture

vanity, I think we did our pairts'. They most certainly did.

Two other eye-witnesses, Hare and Blackader, were in no doubt at all but that God had gotten them the victory. 'A divine Providence', says Hare, 'visibly assisted us from the beginning to the end of this action and afforded us such helps as were above all human choice or appointment; as particularly in our first coming up there was such a mist as did not incommode us at all but was sufficient to hide the march of the army so that the enemy saw nothing but our advanced squadrons; and it does not appear that they thought of seeing anything more, insomuch that when they discovered our whole army they were all in a hurry and consternation, while our troops came up with their usual heartiness and alacrity of aggression. Besides, the sun and wind were with us during the most difficult and critical disputes, which were no small advantage to us'.

'We fought a bloody battle', wrote Blackader, 'and by the mercy of God have obtained one of the greatest and completest victories the age can boast of . . . I believed firmly that His angels had me in charge and that not a bone should be broken'. For all that he had sustained 'a small touch of a wound in the throat', but at least he was not 'groaning with broken bones or bullets in the body, as many are'. To these, on the battlefield and later in hospital at Nördlingen, he gave what comfort he could, albeit with heavy moralising, which it is to be hoped he kept to his journal.

Lediard says that at the end of that stupendous day Marlborough had been in the saddle for sixteen hours - Marlborough himself made it seventeen hours.

III

AFTERMATH

9

Conclusion

'And everybody praised the Duke
Who this great fight did win'.
'But what good came of it at last?'
Quoth little Peterkin.
'Why, that I cannot tell', said he,
'But 'twas a famous victory'.
                SOUTHEY, *After Blenheim*

The sun was setting as Marlborough gave orders for dressing the wounded and getting them under cover. Many a man must have bled to death for want of first-aid. Not till next day could the ten-mile journey by cart to Nördlingen be attempted; and then, what with perils by surgeons and perils by sepsis, one wonders how many survived. Blackader, 'riding all day alone into Nördlingen', two days after the battle, consoled himself with the ninety-first psalm. Reaching the walls of the town by night, he found good lodging and welcoming friends. Next day his wound gave some trouble, but he busied himself among those worse off in the hospital and spent the Sabbath 'in the house of mourning, burying a friend'. This of course produced the gloomiest reflections: 'To see a poor creature on a deathbed, on the brink of eternity, forced to quit the hold of all earthly comforts - nothing but horror, nothing comfortable to look to in the other world - surrounded with jolly companions, miserable comforters, is very affecting. Then a view of Christ is precious, an interest in Him is worth a thousand worlds'. True enough. Yet at such a time might not a few jolly companions prove of more comfort than one stern and disapproving Presbyterian?

At the Schellenberg alone the allied wounded were

estimated at nearly 4,000 to which were added 7,525 from Blenheim. To care for these there were at most nine surgeons and their mates, two physicians and two apothecaries, plus amateur-nurses, all supervised by Hudson and his two clerks. At a time when Queen Anne herself, a 'perfect cripple', was being dosed with oil of millipedes, one wonders what was prescribed for the wounded and what sort of nursing those widows went in for. Hare writes glowingly of 'the extraordinary care of the inhabitants of that place (Nördlingen), as well as of our own commissary, physicians and surgeons'. At least it was something that there was a hospital at all and a commander who cared about it.*

There were of course no anaesthetics for amputations. Ten days after the battle Captain Windham of Wyndham's regiment of Horse (6th Dragoon Guards) wrote to his mother, from Nördlingen:

> I was loth to write very soon after the first account I gave you of my being shot in the leg in the late engagement, because truly my surgeons could not tell what to think of the matter; but upon my arrival at this place, which is the hospital for all our wounded, I have got all the help I can desire, and on Tuesday last was a fortnight my leg was doomed to be cut off and accordingly was that day, since which time I thank God there has not happened the least ill accident there could be . . . Surely a greater victory was never gained. They were 11,000 Foot stronger and we were 5,000 stronger in Horse. They were so strongly encamped that they laughed to see us coming.

Captain Windham, reported killed at Blenheim, returned one-legged to the army, to serve at Ramillies and at Malplaquet.

---

* After Blenheim Marlborough insisted that Commissioners for Sick and Wounded should henceforth accompany the army to organise the care of the victims of battle. Chandler: *Marlborough As Military Commander*.

As for the prisoners - some 14,000 of them, needing to be guarded and fed - they soon became a burden and an embarrassment. Blackader and Milner were among those detailed to stand guard over them all night after the battle. 'They were kept enclosed in a lane or hollow square', Blackader remembered, 'formed by the troops at the village of Blenheim'. 'The prisoners stood all night and . . . the officers thereof the Duke out of compliment allowed to wear their swords', adds Milner.

The rest of our men lay on their arms all night in the field of battle, the left of the lines being at Sonderheim and the right towards Mörslingen. It was just as well that next morning they found plenty of booty. In those of the enemy's tents which had been left standing (some had been bundled away to Höchstädt) there were 'great quantities of herbs and vegetables; and nearer to the Danube there lay about one hundred fat oxen ready skinned, which were to have been delivered out this day to the French troops'. They would last a day or two, but as Marlborough well knew, the whole hungry host must soon be on the move. In the meantime, says Saint-Simon, Marlborough 'treated them all, even the humblest [of his prisoners], with the utmost attention, consideration and politeness, and with a modesty perhaps more distinguished than his victory'.

After the French prisoners had been separated from the rest and sent to the rear, Hare was asked by Churchill to make a list of their officers' names. Having done this, he 'went into a room where were at least sixty or seventy officer-subalterns, of which some were blaming the conduct of their own generals, others walking with their arms folded, others were laid down lamenting their hard fortune and complaining for want of refreshment, till at last, abandoning all reflections of this nature, their chief concern was for their King, abundance of these muttering and plainly saying, "Oh que dira le Roi!"' What indeed! When the news reached him, Louis at first forbade all mention of it. The defeat was unprecedented, unthinkable, unmentionable.

*

'From first to last', writes Chandler, 'Marlborough was the proponent of the major battle as the sole means to break an enemy's military power and thus his will to resist'.* France had been beaten and soundly beaten in her first major defeat for more than forty years. Twenty thousand had been killed or wounded†; fourteen thousand, headed by a Marshal of France, taken prisoner; not to mention the loss of sixty cannon and three hundred standards and colours: a shattering reverse from which it would take the French army at least five years to recover. 'From Blenheim', wrote Belloc, 'dates the retreat of the military power of France'.

The post mortem on the battle (as of course after every great battle) has continued for more than two and a half centuries and seems likely to last until Armageddon; after which, presumably, the debate may go on in a better world, and with further enlightenment. In the meantime the rights and wrongs of Blenheim have been filtered through many minds, some wise, some prejudiced. We have the evidence of those who were there; Parker and Milner, Hare and Blackader, Orkney and Mérode-Westerloo, and of quite a few more, both on the winning and the losing sides. And these have been succeeded by critics, poets and historians, by Swift, Addison, Lediard, Burnet, Coxe, Macaulay, Churchill, Trevelyan and the rest.

Trevelyan surpasses himself in his description of the most critical moment of the day:

> At last the hour of decision had come. The confused fighting in the centre all that afternoon had brought the allied line forward some little distance from the Nebel.

---

* Chandler: *Marlborough As Military Commander.*
† The British and their allies lost 12,500 casualties.

The French infantry there had been reduced to a handful of boys who knew nothing of battles except how to die at their post. The French squadrons were fighting as separate units rather than as a single force; after many a gallant charge they were becoming tired and the flame of their first confidence had burnt out. Tallard had joined them at last, but he was not the man to put spirit or order into their ranks.

Such was the condition of the centre when, about five o'clock, Marlborough marshalled the English and allied cavalry in one magnificent line for the decisive charge. His orders were that they should advance at a smart trot that would enable them to keep their ranks thigh to thigh, but a trot that was to get faster as they approached the enemy with drawn swords and no firearms in hand. The French, instead of charging in the same style, halted to 'present their fusils'. Their disunited and disheartened squadrons were engulfed and borne along in the trot that soon broke into a gallop for dear life on one side, for hot revenge on the other. In the heave of that resistless wave the thinned ranks of the infantry recruits vanished, like a child's castle on the sands melting in the wash of waters.

Far to the north, on the hills above Lutzingen, along the battle-stained edge of the fir forest, Prussian, Dane and Austrian, French and Bavarian, in the intervals of their charges and countercharges, stood straining their eyes southward over the battlefield, which they alone of the combatants could see in its entirety. Four miles away their vision was bounded by the pillar of battle-smoke which concealed the spire of Blenheim. At the supreme moment of the day those eager spectators on the hillside had seen the two waves of opposing cavalry approach, meet and mingle into one long, locked line of combat; then, in an ecstasy of suspense, they had watched it heave, bend, break and scatter to the west. The remoter distances of the plain soon appeared to be sprinkled with innumerable moving spots, all making, like insects in desperate haste, towards the brushwood line of the Danube or the tall, sentinel Schloss of Höchstädt. In those few minutes the watchers on the hills had seen the turn of the tide in Europe, the ebb of the highwater mark of King Louis' effort for universal monarchy.*

Others, including Lord Acton and Hilaire Belloc, have been critical of Marlborough's tactics, and more especially of his attack on the village of Blenheim, with great loss and small success, at the beginning of the battle. Sir Winston Churchill has risen to that challenge:

> Marlborough's part throughout was to conquer the French right and centre. This he could only do by carrying the main body of his army across the Nebel between Blenheim and Oberglau and outfighting Tallard on the open plain. It would be a great help to him to capture Blenheim, and he assuredly bid high for the prize. But if he had taken Blenheim in the early afternoon he could never have moved the mass of his army through the village or across the water-meadows between it and the Danube. There would still have remained the task, so full of danger, of bringing his army across the Nebel and forming a line of battle beyond it. Short of the capture of Blenheim, nothing could help him more in this than the attracting into the village of the largest number of French infantry. For either purpose he must make the same kind of furious attack which he had led on the enemy's right at the Schellenberg. But the failure to storm the village required no alteration in his general plan. As we have seen, only one brigade of infantry and a few squadrons of cavalry were withdrawn from Cutts' command, and these used to wall off the enemy in Blenheim from interfering with the main advance, which once it began proved, as Marlborough had expected,

* G. M. Trevelyan: *England Under Queen Anne* Volume I: *Blenheim* (Longmans).

irresistible. There was therefore no change of the plan, which in fact unfolded methodically, hardly modified at all by the convulsions of battle.

The one great hazard which Marlborough was forced to run was the crossing of the rivulet and its marshes. On this his judgment and much else were staked. He achieved it by the peculiar tactical arrangement of his lines of Horse and Foot, which arose from his understanding of the new power of firearms. It should not be assumed that Tallard could have prevented the passage by attacking earlier with his whole cavalry. He might well have worn them out against the fire of the steady and well-trained infantry of Marlborough's first line. Yet this operation and the passage of the Nebel were at once the main, the most original and the most dangerous part of the plan. When in the morning Eugene rode off to attack the much larger numbers of Marsin's army, and thought also of the task which his comrade must perform or perish, he may well have felt that their burden had been fairly divided.*

Belloc on the whole, praises Marlborough, not least for his march to the Danube, which forced the French to reinforce hurriedly with raw troops, over-marched and poorly provisioned. His own cavalry, even after their long journey, were in good trim; his gunners were better trained. 'Artillery', adds Belloc, 'did not yet decide battles; but Marlborough and Eugene, in fire-value, wiped out the numerical superiority of the French in guns, nine to five'.†

Today the most recent commentator, David Chandler, is convinced that the allies' victory at Blenheim was as much a vindication of their fighting methods as a demonstration of the talents of their commanders. He goes on to say:

---

* Winston S. Churchill: *Marlborough: His Life and Times* Vol. I (Harrop).

† Marlborough brought sixty guns on seven barges up the Rhine, field-artillery which gave good service at Blenheim; but his army was short of siege guns and could muster only thirty for Ingoldstadt.

The proper use of fire and movement, the controlled platoon-volleys, the effect of cold steel wielded by the cavalry, the careful siting of batteries, all contributed to the downfall of the French army, which obstinately clung to the outmoded tactics of a former age . . . But the chief credit for the victory was due to Marlborough's generalship: his firm control of the battle at its different stages, his personal intervention at the places of crisis and his proven ability to weld a multi-national army into an integrated weapon of high morale and single-minded purpose, which contrasted most markedly with Tallard's muddled leadership and weak authority. In Prince Eugene the Duke was fortunate to find a kindred spirit, willing to co-operate to the full in accepting Marlborough's overall direction of the struggle. He was equally fortunate in his subordinate generals and in the calibre of the men they led.*

It was indeed the man they followed who counted as much as - and in many a case more than - the cause. As Belloc puts it:

The great captain may be judged by the light in the eyes of his men, by the endurance under him of immense fatigues; by the exact accomplishment of one hundred separate things a day, each clearly designed and remembered, by his grasp of great sweeps of landscape, by his digestion of maps and horizons, and finally and particularly by this - that the great captain, whether he loses or wins, risks well: he smells the adventure of war and is the opposite of those who, whether in their fortunes or their bodies, chiefly seek security. Judged by all these tests, John Churchill Duke of Marlborough was a supreme commander; and it is not the least part in our recognition of this that the first and chief of the great actions upon which his fame reposes was an action essentially and

* Chandler: 'The Campaign of 1704 ('History Today' January 1963).

typically hazardous and one the disastrous loss of which was as probable as or more probable than the successful issue which it obtained.*

Tallard, on his way under escort to Frankfurt, reflected that things would have been still worse had Marlborough maintained the pursuit. Most of Marsin's and the Elector's men had escaped.

Our French general who was fortunate enough to be among those who got away, concludes his dispatch from Strasbourg:

> When Monsieur de Marsin saw the Horse of his right and ours routed, he bethought himself of retreating with his left, which through the cares of Comte de Bourg had always repulsed the enemy, having charged them as they passed. He drew off all his infantry and marched leisurely as far as the morass of Höchstädt, which he repassed in good order and came to Dillingen, where the resolution was taken to send all the Horse to Ulm, by Goldenfingen, and to cause all the baggage to pass the Danube during the night.
>
> In the morning we drew up all the infantry and came to encamp at Lipent, leaving a thousand men at Lauingen with orders to retreat as soon as the enemy should approach and to burn the bridge, which was done; and marching since with precipitation we bring to the King the poor remains of an army, grieved to death, and which is no otherwise guilty than through the non-performance of the positive order which had been given not to let the enemy pass the rivulet, and to charge them as they passed, altogether and not by brigades, as we did against a body formed and formidable, which at last penetrated into our centre and surrounded the infantry.

Tallard was the scapegoat but, in his view, he had nothing

* Belloc: *Blenheim.*

to reproach himself with. He had foreseen disaster and had tried to prevent it. Even so, he wished he could have died at his post. 'Please remember', he wrote, 'I had only thirty-six battalions and forty-four squadrons, having had to double my squadrons because of the death of the horses [from disease caught in Alsace]. I was attacked by forty-four battalions and eighty-nine squadrons'. In his opinion there were three reasons for the defeat: 1. The *Gendarmerie* failed to repulse the five English squadrons. 2. Marsin's right and Tallard's left were unable to crush their opposing forces before they were reinforced. 3. The second line of cavalry, both on the left and on the right, were unsuccessful, and the second line of infantry were abandoned. Most of the cavalry, he added, did badly, 'I would say very badly'. He makes no mention of the Nebel, of which Hare says: 'The French are blamed for nothing in their conduct but in not bringing their troops down to the rivulet to hinder our passing it, which our generals all blame them for, and their own officers that we have prisoners agree in it'. Nor does Tallard refer to his army's vast superiority in the number of cannon.

In the opinion of Mérode-Westerloo, who was Flemish, the French lost the battle through over-confidence and contempt of the enemy, through faulty field-dispositions and through inexperience and indiscipline, more especially among Tallard's troops.

Among the aristocrats who had commanded French regiments there were of course plenty to lay all the blame, and with some reason, on Tallard; but Louis himself, to whom Marlborough had allowed Tallard to write, was magnanimous enough, once over the first shock, to say he sympathised and felt for him in the loss of his son, who had died of wounds.

Stressing the disadvantage of a divided French command, Belloc wrote:

On the field of Blenheim, command upon the allied side was divided, but the division was neutralised by two important factors: first, that Eugene was of one mind and soul with Marlborough; secondly, that Marlborough was a man of exceptional tact in managing to retain the reality of undivided generalship under the surface of a divided one. From the day when the strange arrangement had been come to in the Neckar valley that he and Baden should command on alternate days, much earlier in all his negotiations with the Dutch, and here in the very decision of the campaign, he managed so to behave that at the critical moment his will should be the deciding will.

The enemy, on the other hand, were divided not only in their councils and methods but in their dispositions; so that 'in effect the French left under Marsin and the Elector was one army, with its cavalry upon either extremity of the line; while the French right, though it had no cavalry on its extreme right, was another army, with cavalry on its left wing . . . and the French centre was filled with Horse, where it had far better have been filled with Foot . . . Blenheim', concludes Belloc, 'was a cavalry battle won by cavalry and its effect was clinched by cavalry. The poor role played by the guns was characteristic of the time: the cannon as a mobile weapon had yet to be understood'. As for Marlborough, 'Risk was in the temperament of the man; and it is a temperament which in warfare accounts for the greatest things'.

*

In a manuscript volume labelled 'Camp Reports', at Blenheim Palace, the entry for August 13th, 1704, consists of a single line, neatly written:

Fought the battle of Blenheim and lay in the field all night.

Marlborough spent the night after the battle in a water-mill near Höchstädt. In Höchstädt itself the castle still held six hundred of the enemy, who surrendered next day. There is a story that the English would have moved in on the evening of August 13th, had they not mistaken tombstones in the churchyard, glinting in the setting sun, for the cuirasses of the French.

Francis Hare waited, to write to his cousin, on the following day. He then sent a graphic account beginning: 'For want of paper I can give you but a short account of the greatest victory that has been won in the memory of man . . .' It was the Marlborough touch.

Dr Coxe tells us that the next day Marlborough rode over the battlefield and saw the dead. In his letter from Höchstädt dated August 14th Marlborough asked Secretary Harley to let him know the Queen's pleasure in the matter of the prisoners, and added: 'I should likewise be glad to receive Her Majesty's directions for the disposal of the standards and colours, whereof I have not yet the number but guess there cannot be less than a hundred, which is more than has been taken in any battle these many years'. In the meantime, in the tracks of Parke, he sent Lord Tunbridge to the Queen to give her a full account of the battle.

On August 17th, writing from Steinheim to the other Secretary of State, Sir Charles Hedges, Marlborough again refers to the prisoners now added to daily by deserters and fugitives. 'They are not only very troublesome', he says, 'but oblige us to continue here while we should be pursuing our blow and following the enemy, who are retired towards the Iller. We are endeavouring to persuade Prince Louis to quit the siege [of Ingoldstadt] and come and join us . . .' There was no difficulty there, for Ingoldstadt could now be left to capitulate; but would Baden ever forgive them for his absence from Blenheim and his lost share of the glory? He would not.

'Had the success of **Prince Eugene been** equal to his merit',

Blenheim church

The original course of
the Danube today near
Sonderheim with banks
'two pikes high' where
French cavalry drowned

Blenheim village occupied and barricaded by the French

The Earl of Orkney

Lord Cutts

wrote Marlborough to his duchess, the day after Blenheim, 'we should in that day's action have made an end of the war'. To which Hare adds, in his journal: 'The Imperial Horse behaved themselves very ill and if my Lord had not suc- coured them, had lost the day'. Yet there were and still are those who would give Eugene the lion's share of the kudos for winning the victory. Perhaps like Marlborough's royalist father, and like Marlborough himself after 1710, Eugene had been faithful but unfortunate. 'At Blenheim he learnt to appreciate Marlborough as a general, and there was glory enough for both. Afterwards the two men worked in perfect harmony marred by no twinge of jealousy'.*

Four days later Marlborough was again writing to his wife. Since the battle he had been so ill, he told her, he had had to be bled. The French had surrendered Augsburg and so had abandoned Bavaria and retreated to Ulm, the allies' next objective. 'This day', he added, 'the whole army has returned their thanks to Almighty God for the late success, and I have done it with all my heart; for never victory was so complete, notwithstanding that they were stronger than we, and very advantageously posted . . .'

While the allies were celebrating with *feux de joie*, the enemy's retreat to Ulm was nightmarish. At Lauingen, where Marsin had spent all night building two bridges, there was, according to Mérode-Westerloo, complete chaos. He himself, bypassing Lauingen with the cavalry, was thirty hours in the saddle without sleep or food and with only one drink of water. The plight of the infantry was worse and a great many deserted, 'finding', as Hare says, 'that there was no safety in the country, but that their comrades were killed by the peasants in every village they came to'. The wounded of course were the worst off of all. Bavarian officers burned their own coaches and waggons to free the horses for litters to carry off more than a thousand wounded

* Francis: *op. cit.*

123

officers and six thousand others. 'A great many of them', adds Hare, 'never reached so far as Ulm, for . . . most of the villages our army marched through were full of new graves'.

Of those that did reach Ulm Mérode-Westerloo says he found some in a penniless condition and had them looked after in his own quarters while he himself slept in a tent. His own wounds forgotten, though he had a knee the size of a man's head, he was in splendid spirits, having just been assured by the Elector that he was the only man to have come out of that sad battle well. 'At this time', he adds (August 21), 'we heard of the fall of Ingoldstadt and of Prince Louis of Baden's rage when he learned of the trick Prince Eugene and the Duke of Marlborough had played him'.

*

Parke galloped across Europe, spreading the good news as he went. From Frankfurt Henry Davenant wrote to George Stepney, our Ambassador in Vienna: 'Yesterday Colonel Parke came here with the agreeable news of the victory we have gained over the enemies. This battle will in all appearance put an end to the war in the Empire and give the means of assisting the Duke of Savoy, who is very near his ruin. The Duke of Marlborough has beyond all dispute saved the Empire. Affairs were in no very good condition before this engagement'. And to Secretary Harley: 'The people here confess that they owe to the Duke of Marlborough and to our troops the safety of Vienna.'

Even so, England had to wait eight days (three of them were spent in crossing the Channel) for her news of the victory. Sarah, at St James's, after reading the note, sent Parke on to Windsor, where Queen Anne sat in the bay of the long gallery overlooking the terrace. Some say she was at dominoes with Prince George. Of course she was overjoyed. But first, rewards for the messenger (her miniature and a thousand guineas); and then orders for bells and bonfires, and a quick note to Sarah:

I have had the happiness of receiving my dear Mrs Free-man's by Colonel Parke, with the good news of this glorious victory which, next to God Almighty, is wholly owing to dear Mr Freeman, on whose safety I congratulate you with all my soul.

The Duchess was showered with congratulations. 'I do not wonder you are all joy', wrote the Bishop of Salisbury's wife, Mrs Burnet, 'The Bishop said he could not sleep, his heart was so charged with joy. He desires your Grace would carefully lay up that little letter'*

Perhaps one of the most moving and least literate notes Marlborough received was from the Queen's Danish Prince Consort: 'Tho' I can not expres my self soe well as others', Prince George assured him, 'my hart is with all truth yours'.

---

* Marlborough's dispatch, though fading, is still to be seen in the first stateroom at Blenheim Palace.

10

After Blenheim

Where will he next the flying Gaul defeat
To make the Series of his Toils complete?
ADDISON, *The Campaign*

'I shall say nothing as to the consequences that attended this famous battle', wrote Richard Kane, 'more than that it decided the fate of the Empire, fixed the Imperial Crown in the House of Austria and was the first fatal blow that Louis XIV had received during his whole reign'.

In London few counted the cost – why should they? – for never had there been such a month for victory as that August, by land and sea. On the 4th Admiral Rooke had taken Gibraltar and on the 24th, in a long and bloody battle, he and the Dutch had beaten the French off Malaga. There were bells, bumpers and bonfires. The very mention of Tallard in Marlborough's coach called for another round. The loyal citizens of London emptied its cellars.

At another level the Queen called for a national thanksgiving on September 7th and in her coach-and-eight drove to St Paul's, 'None with her but the Duchess of Marlborough in a very plain garment, the Queen full of jewels'. It was, adds John Evelyn, 'one of the most serene and calm days that had been all the year'. On the roof of the cathedral a flag was run up as a signal to the Tower gunners to synchronise their salvo with the choir's bursting into the Te Deum.

In his sermon the Dean, Dr Sherlock, deftly awarded credit for the victory to a miraculous providence, swayed and won over by the devotion, justice and bounty of a pious queen. For who could deny but that 'a truly devout, praying, just and charitable Prince must be an overmatch when the Divine Providence espouses the quarrel'? 'Your Majesty', he went on to remind her, 'has lately made a very acceptable oblation to God of the first fruits and tenths for the augmentation of small vicarages. This directly tends to the glory of God in providing for His ministers ... Now God has expressly declared: Them that honour me I will honour and those who despise me shall be lightly esteemed. And I know not why we may not reasonably conclude that this great honour God hath bestowed on Your Majesty is a visible testimony of His acceptance of your pious offering.'

So much for the listening Queen. Marlborough, in his absence, might then be treated with condescension. 'God does not act immediately by Himself', the Dean told his audience, 'but chooses fit instruments to execute His wise and gracious designs; and if He does not find them every way fit, He makes them so, and if he raises them somewhat above the common standard of nature, this is a new addition to their glory. But whether it was nature or something supernatural, certainly never was man better fitted with courage, conduct and unwearied industry for so great an enterprise, and the success answered it all . . .'

Sarah, in waiting on the Queen, thought the sermon 'an heap of Bombast' and was glad Marlborough was not there to hear it; and for his part as he said himself, while troubles lasted he must have his share of them; some might say more than his share. Even now, after his greatest victory, he was to be hobbled and thwarted. The Emperor Leopold, not ungrateful for his deliverance (though there had been that solemn invocation, prescribed by himself), again offered him a princedom, but made no mention of a principality to go with it. Even the obelisk Leopold proposed to raise on the battlefield, as a lasting memorial, never seems to have been set up, although Lediard says it was. But most frustrating of all, after agreeing to the siege of Landau, the Emperor failed to support it with ammunition or money; nor were matters improved by the arrival of his second son, the amiable King of the Romans, who came to 'conduct' the siege and whose authority was resented by the Margrave of Baden. Not surprisingly, though Ulm had fallen on September 11th and released some guns, Landau held out until November 28th.

Though never one to show his feelings, least of all to his men, Marlborough in his letters shared some of them with his closest friend in England, Lord Godolphin. On August 17th he told him: 'Ever since the battle I have been so employed about our own wounded men and the prisoners that I have not had one hour's quiet, which has so disordered me that if I were in London I should be in my bed in a high fever'. And eight days later:

> I am suffered to have so little time to myself that I have a continual fever on my spirits, which makes me very weak; but when I go from hence I am resolved to go in my coach till I come to the Rhine, which I do not doubt will restore me to perfect health. Nothing but my zeal for her Majesty's service could have enabled me to have gone through the fatigues I have had for the last three months; and I am but too sure when I shall have the happiness of seeing you, you will find me ten years older than when I left England. I do not say this to complain, for I esteem myself very happy if I can make any return for her Majesty's goodness to me and mine.

In organising the return from Blenheim the admirable Adam Cardonnel was in correspondence with Hudson the commissioner at Nördlingen.

'My lord Duke is well pleased to find your hospital in such good order', Cardonnel tells Hudson but, he adds regretfully, no more surgeons can be spared for it. After Blenheim Marlborough was planning to set up another hospital at Mayence, 'for as the Army is like to make some stay on the Rhine, we may have occasion for it, though I hope not much'. In the meanwhile Hudson was 'not to stir from Nördlingen without my lord Duke's particular directions'. On September 19th Cardonnel again wrote to Hudson:

His Grace is pleased to order that you break up your hospital at Nördlingen as soon as you can get waggons enough to carry off your stores and such of the sick and wounded men as may be transported without danger, and make the best of your way to Mayence. When you come to Werthen I suppose the country will be very glad to furnish you with boats to carry you down the river, to save the expense of waggons, which will likewise be much easier to you and the men . . . Leave such officers and attendants with the medicines for the men that cannot be removed from Nördlingen as may be absolutely necessary . . . Some careful sergeants must be left behind to conduct them.

And on October 17th:

My lord Duke commands me to acquaint you that the disabled soldiers who have lost their limbs and cannot be capable of any further service must be continued upon the regiment's charge until his Grace's arrival in Holland, when he will give further orders concerning them. As for the widows, they must go down in the boats and as soon as they arrive in Holland should have five gilders each to carry them home. When they come into England, each widow should likewise have a little note from you to Mr Vanderpol to give them their passage.

His last note, dated November 10th, is personal:

His Grace recommends to you the care of his wine and to embark his calache if it comes in your way. I need not recommend my wine to you, but pray let my cask from the Elector be well marked. I shall not be much concerned if the Neckar were not come. I give you many thanks for the chocolate.

*

As was to be expected, the coach journey to Landau made Marlborough worse rather than better and he was seized with 'a cold fit of an ague'.

On October 10th he wrote to his duchess: 'I came this afternoon from Landau . . . That siege goes on so very slowly that I can give no guess when it is likely to end . . . For thousands of reasons I wish myself with you . . . I am at this time so very lean that it is extreme uneasy to me, so that your care must nurse me this winter or I shall certainly be in a consumption'. Sarah was alarmed and begged him to retire. He answered:

> If I considered only myself, I agree with you, I can never quit the world in a better time; but I have too many obligations to the Queen to take any resolution but such as [for] her service must be first considered. I hope how-ever in a little time all this business may be so well settled as I may be very easily spared, and then I shall retire with great satisfaction and with you and my children end my days most happily; for I would not quit the world, but be eased of business in order to enjoy your dear company.

He soon recovered and was eager to attack before winter on the Moselle and so leave a direct route into France open for his spring campaign. When Landau failed to fall he left its reduction to others while he, after passing through 'the terriblest country that can be imagined for the march of an army with cannon', took Trèves and Traerbach and left them well-garrisoned for the winter, while he went on a diplomatic mission to Berlin. Though he had not, as he had hoped, reduced Saar Louis, he still, as he told Godolphin, reckoned the campaign well over with the allies' winter quarters on the Moselle, 'which', he added 'I think will give France as much uneasiness as anything that has been done this summer'.

In other directions too burdens were lifted. Under pressure the Emperor found some fifteen square miles of Swabia, called Mindelheim, to support Marlborough's title of Prince of the Holy Roman Empire. It was not much, and ten years later even that was restored to Bavaria. The title and rank however remain in the Marlborough family to this day.

The prisoners had been disposed of: half of them to Eugene, the other half (Marlborough's) being sent to Frankfurt. Tallard, allotted to Marlborough, fell sick on the journey and was allowed to take the waters at Aix.

On December 14th Marlborough landed at Greenwich. With him were Tallard and thirty-five other French officers, none below the rank of Lieutenant-Colonel. After seeing the Queen and depositing in the Tower all the standards and colours his wing of the army had captured at Blenheim, Marlborough went to the House of Lords for a solemn address in which he was told:

Your Grace has not overthrown young, unskilful generals, raw and undisciplined troops but . . . has conquered the French and Bavarian armies, armies that were fully instructed in all the arts of war, select veteran troops, flushed with former victories and commanded by generals of great experience and bravery . . . The exorbitant power of France is checked and, I hope, a happy step made towards reducing of that Monarch within his due bounds and securing the liberties of Europe. The honour of these glorious victories, great as they are, under the immediate blessing of Almighty God, is chiefly if not alone owing to your Grace's conduct and valour. This is the unanimous voice of England and of all her Majesty's allies. This most honourable House is highly sensible of the great and signal services your Grace has done her Majesty this campaign and of the immortal honour you have done the English nation, and have commanded me to give you their thanks for the same.

In his brief reply Marlborough said:

I must beg on this occasion to do right to all the officers and soldiers I had the honour of having under my command. Next to the blessing of God, the good success of this campaign is owing to their extraordinary courage. I am very sure it will be a great satisfaction as well as encouragement to the whole army to find their services so favourably accepted.

On January 3rd the captured standards and colours were carried in triumphal procession from the Tower to Westminster Hall. Officers of the Blues carried the thirty-four French standards; pikemen of the Guards the hundred and twenty-eight French colours. In the City, in the Strand and in St James's, where Queen Anne was watching from Lord Fitzharding's lodgings, they were cheered all the way; and in St James's Park they were greeted with two salvoes of forty cannon, as with banners streaming they marched through to the Hall. Today, of all those standards and colours proudly brought to England not one has survived. At Höchstädt one is shown a standard taken from the hand of a dead cornet, his name and nationality unknown; not one coloured thread is left.

Three days later another procession took Marlborough and his officers to a banquet with the Lord Mayor and aldermen in the Goldsmiths' Hall. 'Already', comments Sir Winston, 'the City of London had risen upon the European scene as a financial and political entity . . . The destruction of the Armada had preserved the life of Britain: the charge at Blenheim opened to her the gateways of the modern world'.

Three giant stepping-stones of victory - Blenheim-

Ramillies-Oudenarde – by alternate years (1704, 1706, 1708) were for all time to establish Marlborough's renown. It was no fault of his that 'from 1705 the Spanish front proved as fatal a drain on the alliance's resources as ever it did to Napoleon a century later',* preventing Marlborough from making a thrust into the heart of France itself to press home the advantage gained at Blenheim; nor that the Treaty of Utrecht, in his view, surrendered most of the fruits of his conquests and played into the enemy's hands. He might perhaps – in 1708, in 1709 – have contrived an earlier peace; but for himself he had no wish to prolong the war.

Nor was it his fault that in his absence abroad his wife unwittingly undermined the Queen's friendship, while those they had supposed their friends – Harley, Abigail Hill and St John – secretly speeded their downfall. Only Fate at her most sardonic could on the one hand have countenanced that sapper-operation and on the other produced a set of circumstances which would leave England with Gibraltar as her most lasting territorial gain from all the tedious campaigns of the Spanish Succession.

*

The thanks and the feasting of January 1705 were proper enough. But for such a conqueror, the man the Queen delighted to honour, should there not be something more lasting, a public monument perhaps, a statue, a London square? Godolphin's own prudent idea of an annual thanksgiving was frowned upon. A munificent sovereign could surely do better than that. And so it was that the royal estate at Woodstock came, with her usual, charming diffidence in giving, to be offered by Anne to the Marlboroughs, still her dearest and closest friends.

---

* Chandler: 'Genius of Blenheim' (*Observer*, 23 July 1972).

11

The Memorial

'The remembrance of which will endure as long as history shall
be wrote or read or even till Time shall be no more . . .'
BISHOP BURNET writing of the battle of Blenheim

Woodstock Manor was in ruins, but it went without saying
that a house worthy of the nation's hero (Blenheim Castle?)
would be built there. And indeed, with the help of the
Queen's skilled officers - surveyor, mason, gardener, master-
carver - diversion might be found in planning every detail
from taming the savage park to reserving a suite on the
garden front for Mr Montgomery: Lord Treasurer Godolphin; and a lodge for Brigadier Cadogan. It was to be a
monument to be lived in - a royal notion indeed! Yet Sir
Winston, who was born there and in time earned a comparable reward, shook his head over Marlborough's acceptance of it:

Marlborough had set his heart upon this mighty house
in a strange manner. Sarah considered it as his 'greatest
weakness'. It certainly gives us an insight into the recesses
of his being. There is no doubt that the desire for pos-
thumous fame, to 'leave a good name to history' . . . was
in these years his strongest passion. At his age he could
not hope to enjoy Blenheim much himself . . . It was as a
monument, not as a dwelling, that he so earnestly desired
it . . . As the Pharaohs built their pyramids, so he sought
a physical monument which would certainly stand, if
only as a ruin, for thousands of years. About his achievements he preserved a complete silence, offering neither
explanations nor excuses for any of his deeds. His answer

was to be this great house. This mood has characterised dynasts in all ages, and philosophers in none. Remembrance may be preserved to remote posterity by piling great stones on one another and engraving deep inscriptions upon them. But fame is not to be so easily captured. Blenheim cost him dear. It weakened him in his relations with hostile ministers. It exposed him to mockery and malice. The liability for its expense was turned as a weapon against him . . . Indeed, his happiness lost much and his fame gained nothing by the building of Blenheim. However, Blenheim stands, and Marlborough would probably regard it as having fulfilled its purpose if he returned to earth at this day.*

The scale and audacity of Marlborough's achievements - at the Schellenberg, at Blenheim, at Ramillies, at Bouchain - will not be disputed. Exceptional as he was, his refusal to explain - to write and re-write his self-vindication, as Sarah did - and his leaving instead a house to speak for him is in itself exceptional and in marked contrast with the practice of commanders of more recent times.

And so what is there at Blenheim still to speak for him? Murals and painted ceilings: the lines of battle at Blenheim, by Thornhill in the Great Hall; Peace checking a victorious Marlborough, by Laguerre, in the Saloon . . . but those are allegories. The tapestries, 'dictated' by him, are more personal. Ramillies, strangely enough, is missing, but the rest are there, with Tallard's surrender at Blenheim predominant; and though the Flemish weavers took liberties with perspective and with time, the work is superb and the details are fascinating. Moreover, as Sarah said as long ago as 1740, they are or appear to be still 'as fresh as new'.

From the state entrance, with its towering Corinthian columns, one looks northward, between towers and colonnades, encrusted with Gibbons' symbolic sculpture - ducal

* Churchill: *Marlborough, His Life and Times*, II, 754-5.

coronets mounted upon trampled lilies; the British lion savaging the cock of France - to Vanbrugh's gargantuan bridge ('emphatic as an oath') and so to the Column of Victory, topped with Marlborough's statue, holding aloft a winged Victory 'as an ordinary man might hold a bird'.

From the garden front the periwigged bust of Louis XIV, captured by Marlborough at Tournai, stares southward from above the Saloon portico and carries the legend:

EUROPAE HAEC VINDEX GENIO
DECORA ALTA BRITANNO*

- a nice touch. Here, as Mr Laurence Whistler has said, triumph seems to rest in glory. But where is the Military Garden Louis once looked down on and the terraces with their bastions and curtain-walls where, to the tune of fountain and bird-song, Marlborough and his duchess strolled? In the seventeen-sixties the improver's desolating hand destroyed it; so that today the French king looks across a cricket-pitch to Bladon, where that second champion of Europe and biographer of the first, his own ancestor, rests near the church tower.

*

Luckily, Marlborough's walled kitchen-garden where, as he wrote from Flanders, he longed to taste the peaches, has survived; but gardens, even those with mock-fortifications, cannot usually be counted on to last. Henry Wise, Queen Anne's master-gardener, who with Vanbrugh laid out Marlborough's grounds at Blenheim - the avenues, the military garden, the kitchen-garden - was responsible too for a miniature formal-garden for Tallard, banished in comfort to Nottingham (where he is said to have introduced the growing of celery) as a prisoner of state.

There within a tiny compass - 150 feet by 140 at its widest part - Wise packed in everything an exiled Marshal of France

* Europe's champion offers these lofty ornaments to the genius of Britain.

might reasonably wish for: a fountain, a banqueting-house, gravel walks, clipped hedges, courts, steps, terraces, 'borders adorned with plants and flowers' and a pocket-parterre centring upon sunflowers in honour of *le Roi Soleil*. This too of course has vanished; but who shall say that that vanquished prisoner, at ease in his toy garden or with his friends (he had many) sipping champagne in his summer-house, was not more to be envied than his conqueror, heaping up ever fresh laurels in Flanders while favour ebbed at home, and all at the expense of spirit and of health? Tallard returned to France in 1711 and lived for a further seventeen years.

While Harley, St John and others schemed for peace Marlborough, like Tallard, enjoyed 'a sort of exile', returning to England from Antwerp the day after Queen Anne died, in 1714. 'My Lord Duke', was George I's greeting, 'I hope that your troubles are now all over'. They were not of course. There was ill health. There was bereavement. But at least, in the company of his wife and his doctor, he could visit Bath and Tunbridge; or ride alone in Blenheim Park.

Blenheim Palace, founded in the summer of 1705, was not ready to be lived in until 1719 when Marlborough's health, after cerebral strokes, was broken and he had only three years to live. Towards the end he spoke seldom and with some difficulty; but the story goes that, staring one day at the portrait Kneller had long ago painted of him in armour, he shook his head and said, 'This was once a man'.

He died at Windsor Lodge, in 1722.

Of the rest of the Blenheim cast some were a good deal luckier than others. Marsin died in 1706; Lord Cutts, Colonel Blood and the Margrave of Baden in 1707; General Churchill in 1714; Cadogan in 1726; Tallard and Blackader ('ready to go when called') in 1728; Eugene in 1736; Orkney in 1737; Sarah Duchess of Marlborough in 1744.

Colonel Parke, two years after he had ridden across Europe with the news of Blenheim, was made Governor of

Leeward Islands. During an insurrection in Antigua he killed the ringleader, but was himself murdered soon afterwards in his own house.

Maximilian Emanual, Elector of Bavaria, after being exiled by the Emperor to France, was in 1714 restored to his possessions and built a palace called Schleissheim near Munich. For this he ordered from the same Brussels looms which had woven Marlborough's hangings for Blenheim Palace a set of battle-tapestries in which he himself figured as the hero. Five of these panels were almost identical with the Blenheim *Victories* and had obviously been copied from the same cartoons. 'We can only wonder', adds the author of *The Marlborough Tapestries*, 'at the grim humour and perhaps cynical indifference of De Vos [the weaver], which has led this substitution of the Elector's portrait for that of his victorious adversary in a series of scenes representing the latter's achievements. That the Battle of Blenheim, which cost the Elector his dominions, should fall into this category seems almost past belief'.* The Elector died in 1736.

Very different was the destiny of Marlborough's chaplain, the ingenious Dr Hare, who became Dean of St Paul's and eventually Bishop of Chichester; and who save Sarah was to say that he had not earned it? True, Robert Walpole told her that Hare had no more religion than the Devil; but since he recommended him to an archbishopric, shortly before his death in 1740, he must surely have found him of some merit. Uncomplainingly Hare had shared Marlborough's rigours on campaign, deploring only the insolence of the French, 'who, where they are masters, make war in a most barbarous manner and after all their pretences to politeness and civility, there is not a nation in Europe but who can teach France humanity'.

While Marlborough was 'exiled' in Flanders in 1713 Hare published tracts in his defence and wrote to him: ' 'tis only because some men are afraid of you that they take so much

---

* Alan Wace: *The Marlborough Tapestries at Blenheim Palace.*

Marlborough writing the Blenheim dispatch after he had been in
the saddle for seventeen hours

Blenheim Palace, from an eighteenth century engraving

The Marlborough monument, Blenheim Palace

pains to make you seem unlovely . . . but as your Grace has for many years been the darling of your country, a little time will make you so again'. And in Sarah's long widow-hood when, without Marlborough to control her, her suspicions and quarrels seemed heading for madness, only Hare as an old friend who had once been her son's tutor had the courage to tell her when and where she was wrong. This was savagely resented. He was 'very brutal'. And why should she of all people deny herself the pleasure of speaking her mind whenever she felt like it? At a time when, as he knew, she was looking for someone to write Marlborough's panegyric, he held up to her the example of Marlborough himself: 'always agreeable in conversation and yet always inoffensive; and whatever resentments he had, suppressed them to that degree as made him universally beloved and the idol, in a manner, of all who had the honour to be near him . . . There was in his whole behaviour', he ended, 'an inimitable sweetness which was not only easy to himself but delightful to others'.

Sarah refused to listen. All her life she had been a fighter – had she not begged to be allowed to join Marlborough at the front? – she was not going to haul down her colours now. Friendless and furious, in that wild unmerciful house called Blenheim, she battled on to try to make order out of 'a chaos only God Almighty could finish'. In her own manner she finished it; and there in the chapel, in white marble, she continues to sit, gazing up in adoration at 'that glorious man', his head forever crowned with laurels. Below them are History and Fame, with pen and trumpet poised. The dragon Envy is crushed by the sarcophagus; while at the foot of all, in bas-relief, Tallard surrenders to Marlborough after the battle of Blenheim.

12

Today

The march concludes, the various Realms are past,
Th' Immortal Schellenberg appears at last.
                              ADDISON, *The Campaign*

The journey today, by plane to Munich and then by train to Donauwörth, though dull is no longer laborious. From the tapestry at Blenheim I had imagined the Schellenberg a small mountain overshadowing a walled town. No more than a steep hill - one can climb it in fifteen minutes - it stands in the wings of Donauwörth, as though withdrawn and waiting to be found.

'Follow a small river', I was told, 'but no, a *little* river, to the new hospital and then, with your back to that hospital, cross the river and advance to the green hill'.

Donauwörth, battered by bombs and now by heavy traffic, its walls vestigial, is still pleasant enough, being encircled by the Danube and the Wernitz; but the stream I followed was no more than a brook running through a small park of limes and willows, where boxes nailed high up against tree-trunks make nesting-sites for redstarts, while children and fountains play on grass and moss.

With one's back to the hospital, the prospect of the Schellenberg (the hill of the bell) is pastoral: between horn-beam hedges and lime trees a narrow meadow rises to a chapel, its cupola, painted terracotta, embowered among trees. Both paths to the chapel are steep, that on the right of the meadow being a *Via Dolorosa* with steps and wayside shrines for the Stations of the Cross.

This too I had never imagined and, as I climbed the left-hand path amid hay-scent and bird-song and distant bells, I found myself wondering just what it was all about. The chapel doors were wide open and the place itself was a white cell with scrubbed pews, white flowers on a plain altar and seemingly little else except for two plain archways flanking the altar. A blackcap sang. The sun streamed in. I had as I thought the chapel to myself; yet hesitated to enter the holy of holies behind the altar, and when I did I had a considerable shock. There in a grotto, prostrate and bleeding upon a white, lace-edged cloth, head tilted back and bearded mouth ajar, was what appeared to be a corpse. The shock of course was deliberate. It was staggeringly dramatic; for no one could suddenly come upon that effigy of the entombed Christ, without a catch of the breath.

Thoughtfully I left the chapel and the Lady chapel beside it and made for the Calvary on its higher plateau. And this too is of telling and dramatic beauty, its very symmetry - two thieves, two Marys - stressing in a strange way the inevitability of tragedy on earth for God and man; though there is also that hint of hope, of love beyond death and of redemption. The *Via Dolorosa* with its 131 steps has of course the Calvary as its culmination and at the foot of the Cross there are benches upon which pilgrims may sink down and pray. The setting is perfect. The light, filtered through lime leaves, falls gently upon victims and mourners, touching here upon a robber, there upon a crown of thorns. Beyond the Calvary the green hill again rises steeply, the grass and moon-daisies intermingled with meadow-clary (*salvia pretensis*), its blue spikes as plentiful here as they are on Blenheim's battlefield.

Perhaps it were as well to climb no further, for instead of woods and fortifications the top of the Schellenberg now has a main road, a motel, two large swimming-baths and a barbed-wired stronghold with *verboten* notices worthy of Goering. There is too an outbreak of suburban villas; and on the side of one of them someone has painted, with some spirit, soldiers in uniforms of 1704. But all this can be ignored as one sits on a bench and looks down over Donauwörth to fields and woods much as they must have been when Marlborough rode through them. From here the country is a vast green saucer, not mountainous. Donauwörth has its two big churches but, except for a gateway or so, has lost its walls, the town spreading beyond them to engulf hamlets such as Berg which, when Blood hid his cannon there, was isolated on its own river-island.

The assault on the Schellenberg, steep as it is and at that time wooded, is not hard to imagine. At the foot of the *Via Dolorosa* there is a notice:

> Over this place, where thousands of soldiers who at the battle of the Schellenberg in July 1704 met a hero's death take their rest, a Calvary was in 1721 erected by the Corporation of Donauwörth.

To which a guidebook to the locality adds:

> The *Via Dolorosa* and Crucifixion group were donated by the citizens of the town in thanksgiving for their safety during the bitter battle on the Schellenberg on the 2nd of July, 1704.

And some there be who have no memorial. No mention is made of the town's commandant, whose withdrawal of the guard from the covered way is said to have made a breach for the Margrave of Baden. He is better forgotten; while those whose blood drenched this hill and whose bones still lie buried here are remembered. Of fort, earthworks, wood, death-angle nothing remains; and on the lower slopes 'the once-jarring battlefield has become a silent, awe-inspiring Golgotha and Field of God'. There is a feeling here of strangeness and timelessness, as though the dead of 1704 were contemporary with Christ, lying wounded behind the altar. Their bones are there, as is the effigy, but they them-

142

selves - 'out beyond the shining of the farthest star' - are infinitely distant and remote.

*

If the Schellenberg has changed, so has the battlefield of Blenheim. The Danube has been diverted and canalised and the marshes have been drained, leaving deserts of vast eternity: an arid plain which seems on every side to go on forever. There is no hedge and, except for rare groves of poplars, there are very few trees. One wonders if, after their tedious march, Marlborough's troops even then found it, with sedge and stubble, a daunting and merciless landscape without cover or refuge, with nowhere for thrush to nest or fox to hide. For a fit man within cannon-shot of the enemy this would be bad enough; for the wounded, in the swelter of summer, worse.

It may be something in the light of Bavaria which makes the distances between villages - compact oases in a green desert - seem greater than they are. Blenheim is less than four miles from Lutzingen; it looks more like ten. Oberglau and Unterglau seem remote from each other, while the Nebel between them, thanks to that teutonic passion for regimenting everything from a man to a millstream, is now a disciplined brook, flowing in a straight channel without marsh or meander. In its directness it is comparable with the single-track railway which, following the old Donauwörth to Dillingen road, runs between banks of wild flowers and grasses straight across the battle plain.

In such a landscape one is grateful for the spire of a church. That at Tapfheim I had hoped to climb, as Marlborough did, to gain some notion of the distant battlefield; but that was forbidden. It was unsafe, I was told, and the key could not be found. Like most Bavarian churches it is decorative; and supposedly from the belfry, with his perspective-glass, Marlborough could just make out, more than five miles off, the enemy tents between Blenheim and

Höchstädt; but from neither of those last towers is much of significance to be seen today.

After climbing the 240 wooden steps to the balcony surrounding the cupola of the church at Höchstädt one sees the *Schloss* and the village, a great deal of featureless country and some light industry. From the spire at Blindheim or Blenheim, enclosed as it is, one looks down through a small window to barns and rickyards and again to a flat countryside; but from neither, in summer, can one see the Danube or the Nebel or anything to remind one of fight or flight. Nor is it easy to picture that conference of marshals within Blenheim's spire or tower, a dark, cramped and awkward stairway, without leads or balcony or ringing-chamber or anywhere at all to sit down and ponder things.

The high white walls of Blenheim churchyard have recently been rebuilt on their old foundation. They bear the inscription: 'Here, on August 13, 1704, Marlborough and Eugene defeated the French and the Bavarians'. The black marble tombstones too are modern; and there is an elaborate memorial not to Marlborough's but to Hitler's war. Apart from these changes however the church, encircled first by its churchyard and next by farms and small houses, though these are no longer thatched, must be much as it was on that other hot day when soldiers stood shoulder to shoulder on the graves, and barn-doors were lifted from hinges to strengthen the barricades.

The village is neat, as are the fields about it with endless rows of potatoes hoed by women with handkerchiefed heads. Oberglau is a distant spire, the woods of Lutzingen are a blur on the horizon. Driving or walking about the battlefield and longing for shade one sees the life of those who cultivate it as of a kind that might well have been approved by Luther. In places the countryside is pretty enough with haycocks and blue salvia and swallowtail butterflies; but tilling the soil there looks primitive, tranquil, tough and unmechanised.

As Belloc noted, the battlefield is to the eye almost even and presents no obstacles of gradient. Blenheim itself, built 'on a slight crest', is now eight hundred yards from the Danube and boasts no hill or eminence; and if, as has been suggested, there was once a ridge running from Blenheim to Oberglau, it must long since have been levelled; there is no trace of it today. 'To talk of a "hill" in the French centre', wrote Trevelyan, 'as several of the narratives do, is liable to mislead readers who have not seen the ground for themselves. The slope up from the Nebel is very gradual indeed. The general aspect is of a vast level plain'.

Certainly, the gradient towards Lutzingen (in three miles the plain rises only sixty feet) is gentle; although as one sits on a terrace there, drinking chilled Moselle, one can at last look down on the battlefield, without having to climb a tower, and imagine Eugene's struggle in bringing his army through dense woods to the line of battle.

Inevitably one is told here the tale of a headless horseman who, riding out of a ghostly river, gallops through Blenheim northward across the battlefield, to vanish within the woods of Lutzingen. On battlefields, as in old houses, invention is ever equal to public demand. Again, near Sonderheim, one sees the steep bank of the Danube's original channel, two pikes high, down which Marlborough 'pushed' so many enemy horsemen; and again the imagination is not helped by the narrow, sluggish stream abandoned there.

Near Höchstädt still stands the mill where Marlborough lodged after the battle and in Höchstädt itself there is a small museum with engravings and bayonets and cannon-balls, these last in two sizes: football and cricketball. On the battlefield itself there is no obelisk; only a small stone cross and another more modern stone-memorial, crudely incised. Indeed, except for that threadbare standard at Höchstädt, taken from the hand of a dead cornet, there is nothing here as significant nor as moving as the Calvary on the Schellenberg or the Column of Victory in Blenheim Park.

At Nördlingen, a pleasant town still to be quietly circumnavigated by the roofed walk running round its medieval walls, the wars of Marlborough seem to have been all but forgotten. In the vast parish-church three wall-tablets speak of Bavarian soldiers killed in 1704; and that is about all. For Marlborough's hospital I was directed to St Salvator, now a church but formerly a convent; only to find that the wounded once billeted there were from the Napoleonic wars; though it is possible of course that it had served the same purpose before. After their appalling journey, wherever in that town they were tended, they must have been thankful to see its turreted walls.

*

Today pilgrims of all nations throng to the grave of a later Churchill at Bladon in Oxfordshire and to the Column of Victory in Blenheim Park. It seems right that they should. Not all of them stop to read, at the base of the column, the long panegyric written (strange irony) by Marlborough's one-time enemy Henry St John, who became Viscount Bolingbroke. Those who do, learn that Blenheim Palace is 'a monument designed to perpetuate the memory of the signal victory obtained over the French and the Bavarians near the village of Blenheim on the banks of the Danube by John Duke of Marlborough, the hero not only of his nation but of his age'. After the preamble the inscription continues:

> The arms of France, favoured by the defection of the Elector of Bavaria, had penetrated into the heart of the Empire. This mighty body lay exposed to immediate ruin. In that memorable crisis the Duke of Marlborough led his troops with unexampled celerity, secrecy, order, from the ocean to the Danube. He saw, he attacked, nor stopped but

to conquer the enemy. He forced the Bavarians, sustained by the French, in their strong entrenchments at Schellenberg. He passed the Danube. A second royal army, composed of the best troops of France, was sent to reinforce the first. That of the Confederates was divided. With one part of it the siege of Ingoldstadt was carried on. With the other the Duke gave battle to the united strength of France and Bavaria. On the second day of August,* one thousand seven hundred and four, he gained a more glorious victory than the histories of any age can boast . . .

And ends:

The French acknowledged their conqueror and sued for peace. These are the actions of the Duke of Marlborough, performed in the compass of few years; sufficient to adorn the annals of ages. The admiration of other nations will be conveyed to latest posterity in the histories even of the enemies of Britain. The sense which the British nation had of his transcendent merit was expressed in the most solemn, most effectual, most durable manner. The Acts of Parliament inscribed on this pillar shall stand as long as the British name and language last – illustrious monuments of Marlborough's glory and of Britain's gratitude.

There had been trouble enough over the building of Blenheim and still more over the paying for it. The Duchess, who raised the monument after Marlborough's death, would stand no more nonsense. That is why every tedious Act of Parliament to do with Blenheim Palace or the Marlborough succession is inscribed in marble on the other three sides of the dado. They are all but unreadable and unread; yet who knows? Once in a thousand years they could be useful.

* Old Style. The adoption by England of the Gregorian Calendar in 1752 changed the date of the battle to August 13.

And so Fame runs full circle. A great victory is won. A palace is named after it, a palace in time to cradle a second hero, again of Marlborough stock. Bisect that palace from north to south and your line runs from Marlborough's Column of Victory, through the Great Hall, near Churchill's birthroom and on to the tower of Bladon church, where Sir Winston is buried. Though there be blood, sweat and tears in the making, one can but admire the neatness with which Destiny ultimately rounds things off.

Appendix I

THE MARCH TO THE DANUBE

British Troops which took part in the March to the Danube and the Battle of Blenheim*

Title in 1714	Later Titles
Lumley's	1st King's Dragoon Guards
Wood's	3rd Dragoon Guards
Cadogan's	5th Dragoon Guards
Wyndham's	6th Dragoon Guards
Schomberg's	7th Dragoon Guards
Lord John Hay's	2nd Dragoons; the Royal Scots Greys
Ross's	5th Dragoons; 5th Royal Irish Lancers
1st Battalion 1st Guards	Grenadier Guards
Orkney's	1st and 2nd Battalions, 1st Foot; the Royal Scots
Churchill's	3rd Foot; the Buffs (East Kent Regiment)
Webb's	8th Foot; the King's (Liverpool) Regiment
North and Grey's	10th Foot; the Lincolnshire Regiment
Howe's	15th Foot; the East Yorkshire Regiment
Derby's	16th Foot; the Bedfordshire and Hertfordshire Regiment
Hamilton's	18th Foot; the Royal Irish Regiment
Rowe's	21st Foot; the Royal Scots Fusiliers
Ingoldsby's	23rd Foot; the Royal Welsh Fusiliers
Marlborough's	24th Foot; the South Wales Borderers
Ferguson's	26th Foot, the Cameronians (the Scottish Rifles)
Meredith's	37th Foot; the Hampshire Regiment

Also the Artillery and Engineers.

* Reprinted by kind permission of the publishers, George G. Harrap & Company Ltd. from Sir Winston Churchill's *Marlborough, His Life and Times*, volume I, page 751.

Appendix II

DISCIPLINE FOR HORSE AND FOOT

Discipline of Horse - It is sufficient for them to ride well, to have their horses well managed and trained up to stand fire; that they take particular notice what part of the squadron they are in, their right and left-hand men and file-leaders, that they may when they happen to break readily know to form . . . That they march and wheel with a grace and handle their swords well, which is the only weapon our British Horse make use of when they charge the enemy; more than this is superfluous. The Duke of Marlborough would allow the Horse but three charges of powder and ball to each man for a campaign, and that only for guarding their horses when at grass and not to be made use of in action.

Discipline for a Regiment of Foot - Let us suppose our battalion drawn up with the army on the field of battle, three deep, their bayonets fixed on their muzzles, the Grenadiers divided on the flanks, the officers ranged in the front; and the Colonel or Lieutenant-Colonel on foot, with his sword drawn in his hand, about eight or ten paces in the front, opposite the centre, with an expert drummer by him. He should appear with a cheerful countenance, never in a hurry or by any means ruffled, and to deliver his orders with great calmness and presence of mind . . .

As the commanding officer will be exposed to the fire of his own men, as well as that of the enemy, he is to take special care that he keep opposite the two centre platoons while the other parts of the battalion keep firing; and he must also take as great care that when it comes to the turn of the centre platoons to fire that both he and the drummer step aside and return as soon as they have done, otherwise they must fall by their own fire . . .

When the commanding officer finds there is no avoiding coming to battle, he is to order the soldiers to lay down their knapsacks, tent-poles and what is cumbersome, and the sergeant sends them to some place out of the way . . . If we win the day they will be safe; if not, 'tis no matter what becomes of them . . .

And suppose that we drove the enemy out of all their cover and are pursuing them into a plain; the first thing we are to do is to put ourselves in order, lest the enemy's Horse seeing us in confusion come and cut us to pieces. Wherefore, when the Colonel finds the action he's going upon is like to occasion this disorder, he apprises the battalion of it and bids them mind their colours and keep as close to them as possible. The colours ought to be carried by strong men and kept always well advanced, to whom the Colonel gives strict orders to stick close by him whichever way he takes. He also orders two or three of the ablest drummers to keep close by him and at the same time acquaints both officers and soldiers that whenever they hear the drums beat to arms they immediately repair to their colours, and whichever way they find them draw up or front, they are to range . . . The officers range to their proper distance on each side the colours and . . . the soldiers knowing on which side the colours they are and of the officers they follow, will soon fall into their places, and the battalion be formed in a shorter time than can be imagined . . . The drummers are to be divided into three parts, on the right and left, and behind the two centre platoons, all to range in a line with the sergeants, but not to beat without orders . . . Our battalion being thus formed for battle and as it were riveted together so that no soldier can possibly misbehave but there will be an eye presently upon him, and nothing but the want of care and resolution in the officers can make a battalion thus formed miscarry unless overpowered by numbers or some unforeseen accident.

Use of the Drum in Action - It is not every commanding officer that has a voice capable to go through the management of a battalion when in common exercise, much more [*sic*] in the hurry of action. Would it not be a shame for him to order the Major or Adjutant, in the day of battle, to fight the battalion, and he only a cypher at the head of it and pretend he has not a voice to go through it?

Suppose the commanding officer should happen to be killed, the voice of him that supplies his place may be so different from the other's that it may occasion a confusion; whereas the drum is always the same and much easier heard and understood, especially when the men are trained up by and constantly used to it . . . so that, as it often happens in the hurry of action when it is not possible for the voice to be heard, that then the drum will be of the greatest consequence.

Suppose that the signal for battle is given. Upon this the Colonel orders his drummer to beat a ruffle, which is as much as to say *take care*; and then saying something to encourage and excite the men to the performance of their duty. This may seem ridiculous by some, yet I know 'twill animate and raise an emulation among the soldiers, especially when they have a love for their officers. I cannot but take notice of some gentlemen who instead of treating their men with good nature, use them with contempt and cruelty; by which those gentlemen often meet with their fate in the day of battle from their own men . . .

The Colonel having thus spoke cheerfully to the men, he then gives the word *March!* At which time the drummer beats to the march; and when the battalion has got within four or five paces of him, he turns to the enemy and marches slowly down till he finds they begin to fire upon him; upon which he orders his drummer to cease beating, and turning to the battalion gives the word *Halt!* And then orders his drummer to beat a preparative, upon which the six platoons of the first firing make ready . . . and the front rank kneels, placing their butts on the ground by their left feet, where all are to wait for the next word of command or signal of the drum from the Colonel himself . . . and if he finds his voice not sufficient, he then orders his drummer to beat a flam; at which time the front rank drop their muzzles to the ground and the two rear ranks present . . . The platoons being presented, the Colonel orders the drummer to beat a second flam, on which they fire and immediately recover their arms, fall back and load as fast as they can . . .

I will suppose that the enemy has given ground and put themselves on the retreat and are marching off as fast as they can and consequently faster than we can propose to follow and keep our order, which we must not break upon any account; so that all the Colonel can do on this occasion is to keep firing after them so long as his shot will reach them and then leave them to the Horse.

If we have resolution to keep order and avoid hurry, there is no reasonable body of Horse dare venture upon us. It is not to be imagined how the fire of one rank will stop and disorder Horse; and then a second and a third on the heels of it will certainly send them a packing.

Infantry on the March - So soon as the Colonel has sent off his advance-guard he orders the officer of the rear-guard to take care of the baggage or convoy and see that they keep good order in their march and close to the regiment. This officer is also to detach a sergeant and twelve men to keep at a proper distance in the rear of him, and both of them to look sharp lest the enemy may lie in ambush by the advance-guard and come out in hopes of surprising us in the rear, they having no business to think of attacking us but by surprising us on a disorderly march. Nor is it to be conceived what a panic seizes a body of Foot when they are surprised after such a manner. Nothing but confusion attends them on such occasions and they are cut to pieces before they can get into order. Nor on the other hand can it be conceived with what courage and resolution a body of Foot will be animated when they find themselves in good order and posture of defence.*

* Brigadier-General Richard Kane: *The Wars of William III and Queen Anne* (1735).

Acknowledgments

I

For his kindness in allowing me access, in the Long Library at Blenheim, to many manuscripts and books including Dr Hare's *Journal* and the unpublished correspondence of Marlborough's secretary Adam de Cardonnel; for letting me write my first draft of this book in Blenheim Palace, and reproduce portraits, frescoes and tapestries there, I am most grateful to His Grace the Duke of Marlborough.

For expert advice on early-eighteenth-century battle-tactics, arms and uniforms I am greatly indebted to Mr David Chandler, Deputy-Head Department of War Studies, RMA, Sandhurst, author of *Marlborough as Military Commander* and editor of the journals of Captain Robert Parker and the Count of Mérode-Westerloo.

In Bavaria my thanks are specially due to Frau Dr Grohsmann, archivist of Donauwörth, to Herr Dr Diemer, curator of the Höchstädt Museum, and to Herr Bäuml, Blindheim's schoolmaster, who was kind enough to drive me the length and breadth of the battlefield.

For their assistance in connection with Marlborough House I am grateful to Sir Oliver Millar, Mr Charlton, Mr Davies, Mrs Harper, Mr Thorn, Mr Lyndon and Mr Willshire.

Dr Anne Whiteman has been extraordinarily helpful not only with advice and with the loan of books but by introducing me to another learned historian, Mr John Stoye of Magdalen College, Oxford. To both, my thanks.

Among the libraries and print rooms I have found co-operative and rewarding I can but mention the Bodleian Library, the London Library, the British Museum, the Victoria and Albert Museum, the Royal Military Museum, the Ashmolean Museum and the Rijksmuseum in Amsterdam. At Blenheim my thanks are due also to Mr William Murdock, Miss Thomas, Mr Illingworth, Mr Duffie, Mrs Moore and Mr Parncutt. I would like to thank too